Sea Chang[

To Mo

By
Yvonne Downer

My best wishes –
Yvonne Downer.
February 2005.

M. Johnster
41 Park Street
Dry Drayton, Camb. CB3 8 DA

Sea Change
First Edition
Published by DreamStar Books, March 2004

Lasyard House
Underhill Street
Bridgnorth
Shropshire
WV16 4BB
Tel: 00 870 777 3339
e-mail: info@dreamstarbooks.com

Set in 'Garamond'

The events and opinions in this book are true and originate from the author.

Printed and bound in Great Britain by Antony Rowe Ltd

Acknowledgement

To Anne for her encouragement and belief there was a story to tell.

To Simon whose courage remains an inspiration.

To the computer Guru who frequently came to my rescue.

About the author

The middle one of three children, I grew up in Hove and attended various day schools. My parents gave us wonderful summer holidays away from Brighton, including sailing with my father in his seven ton yawl. I was thirteen when war was declared. In 1940 there was a scare that the invasion could be made in the Brighton area so we evacuated to a village at the foot of the South Downs. Our entertainment was cycling along the South Downs to watch 'dog fights' between Spitfires and the enemy. In the spring of 1943, aged seventeen and a half, I joined the W.R.N.S. I worked as a Boats Crew Wren and Leading Wren in a variety of Naval establishments round Portsmouth harbour and the river Hamble. No longer required at the end of hostilities, I was demobilised in December 1945. By this time I was engaged to an R.N.V.R sub-lieutenant, about to leave the Fleet Air Arm.

We married early in 1947. My husband was studying for an engineering degree at Southampton University and we lived in a houseboat at Swaythling. Our son was born in the summer of 1948 and my husband, after his finals, was accepted by the Royal Navy for a long-term commission. Our daughter was born at the end of 1949 and years of traveling as a service family began. We had many moves, including Malta and Norway.

Between 1958 and 1968 I taught Dressmaking, English and Commerce and, as an amateur, bred and showed dogs – Labradors and Cavalier King Charles Spaniels. While living at Chatham, I studied for a Social Work qualification. A posting to N.A.T.O. followed with plenty of skiing and sailing and I began writing articles for magazines. In 1971, we came back to England and I started a career in Social Work, still following my husband when possible. This gave me wide experience working in Portsmouth, London, West Sussex and finally Brighton. I retired in 1990, was involved with Victim Support, counselled at home and took a creative writing course.

My husband retired from the Royal Navy in 1978 and on inherited land in Sussex, we planted seven acres of Mueller-Thurgau vines and built a bungalow. I remained working full time for Social Services and helped at home at weekends! We ran a small bed and breakfast business, a certificated location for caravans and let stables and grazing for horses to help financially. We celebrated our golden wedding in 1998 and by the summer of 1999 we decided it was time to sell up. That autumn we moved to Gosport, familiar from our service days. A Southerly 115 is berthed just down the road and we have time to enjoy those things we missed when tilling the land. As well as sailing, I write a bit, paint a little, sometimes play bridge, garden and walk Pandora, my Cavalier King Charles. Family and friends are welcome visitors.

In recognition of the valuable work of the
Women's Royal Naval Service

Index

Prologue

Catherine left the busy motorway with relief and took a left hand fork which led into a winding country lane. She had left home early so that she would arrive on time. The roads had been particularly busy with summer holiday traffic. Now that she was near to her destination she could afford time to slow down and just remember. There would be changes on the river. Some of the people she had known would not be there. She had been one of the younger ones.

She drove slowly, trying to recognise the way. So many years had gone by, it was hard to remember exactly what it was like. Was this the way she had followed that early summer of 1943 when England had been at war with Germany for three and a half years. She stole a look in the driving mirror and tried to replace the present image of an elderly, grey-haired woman with her previous self, a young girl of seventeen on the threshold of life. Why, her youngest granddaughter had recently celebrated her own eighteenth birthday.

The invitation had come as an intriguing surprise. A long way to travel but it would give her the opportunity to meet up with old friends and a chance to, sadly, remember those who had not survived. Now the W.R.N.S. had been absorbed into the Royal Navy, it would serve as well as a nostalgic farewell to that particular service.

Catherine lost concentration and took a wrong turning. So many houses and small roads, where was she? She stopped at the side of the road to check her map. Uncertainly she took the next road to the right. Suddenly she caught the glint of water through the trees and knew it must be the river.

The houses on either side of the road looked new and would have been built long after the war. She stopped by a track leading between the homes with their neat, well cared for flowerbeds and manicured lawns. It might lead down to the river, there was time to spare and she was so tempted to look again, on her own.

The track became a path and the lush summer grass was damp under the trees. Catherine's smart shoes were inappropriate but she was undeterred. She felt a rising excitement as the old familiar stench of mud assailed her, rising from banks exposed by a falling tide. Suddenly she was through the trees and the river was before her.

She was desperately disappointed, cheated. It was different, not her river. Yachts lay in all directions. A forest of masts, gleaming structures, racing machines and expensive cruisers were packing the fairway. Catherine narrowed her eyes trying to shut out the jostling vessels and reclaim the trotlines of square craft, the flotillas of ships she had known, served and loved. They were plain in her head but could not be superimposed on the changed scene. But time was running out, she would now have to hurry.

Back in the car, she wondered how sensible it was to reawaken the past after so long. She turned the car, as directed, at the small roundabout, not there in her day and followed the line of cars. The convoy moved slowly towards the Hard and H.M.S. Cormorant's celebration of the anniversary of D Day.

Chapter One

It was a still summer evening and the river flowed peacefully through seagrass meadows. The wide ribbon of shining water was empty except for central lines of giant mooring buoys. Their rusty shackles bowed dutifully towards the mouth of the river, all pulled in the same direction by the slow movement of the turning tide.

This was Catherine's first sight of the river to become so important in her life. She had followed the track through the trees and found the tow-path which led to the boats and the Maintenance Yard. The Petty Officer Wren had told her she would not be needed for duty until the next day so it was an ideal time to spy out new surroundings.

The path was sheltered and there was enough heat in the sun to make her navy, serge suit feel hot and uncomfortable. She unbuttoned her jacket and defiantly pulled off her cap, running her fingers through her dark, springy hair. Catherine's journey to this new Base and the following joining routine had been lengthy and exhausting. There had been no time to think about what was happening. On her own now, she felt anxious and wondered how it would all work out.

This place was so different. She screwed her eyes shut against the sun, low in the sky but still brilliant. She wanted, childishly, to open her eyes and be back with Jean and the others. Jean's clear voice came to mind.

"Don't expect it to be at all the same. Combined Ops isn't a bit like Coastal Forces. Not much red tape and not nearly so efficient." There had been a hint of disapproval in her voice. Jean was loyal to the Motor Torpedo and Gun Boats she was used to. Catherine had secretly hoped loss of red tape and efficiency might mean a lower standard of dress for boatscrew wrens. It was a strain forever keeping plimsolls and lanyards white, shirts crisp and bellbottoms creased in the correct places when duty boats had to be cleaned and bilges bailed. Catherine, at seventeen and a half, enjoyed change and had thought she was ready to move on to her second posting in the W.R.N.S. But, after all, would she like this new Base? Why was H.M.S. Cormorant asking for more Wrens to work on the boats? What sort of work did they actually do?

Catherine pushed the doubts firmly away and opened her eyes. She was struck by the swift movement of the river water and the peculiar tangy smell, pungent in the warm air. An open Cutter nosed round the end of a near jetty with a small figure at the helm. Her uncovered hair shone like fire in the setting sun. A second girl, taller, stood in the bows wielding a boathook.

The rising throb of engines spun Catherine round to look down river, towards the sea. A long line of Landing Craft, thrusting blunt prows aggressively through the water, creamed their way into the mouth of the river. She imagined they were coming home after the day's exercise, she was used to the Motor Torpedo Boats doing just that in Coastal Forces. The Craft looked about the same length as the Coastal Force boats but were squarer in design. As the flotillas came closer she made out individual numbers painted in red on their sides.

The river filled as she watched with rising interest. The Cutter, steered by the red-head, was joined by a second boat. The two small boats danced attendance, nosing the cumbersome vessels into position before making them secure to the central line of mooring buoys. Catherine fancied they acted like sheep dogs and were only satisfied when their flock were neatly paired and tethered in a double line down the centre of the river.

Voices carried clearly across the water. Snatches of talk easily heard as moored ships shut down engines. Exchanged greetings and laughter accompanied the sharp click of a boathook as the Cutters picked up passengers bound for the shore.

"Hi there!" A stocky fair haired girl was coming down the tow path towards Catherine. "You must be Catherine Tenant. I'm June." She pulled her right hand out of her trouser pocket and held it out in welcome.

Catherine just had time to take in the girl's frayed bellbottoms, grey gym shoes and cap perched on the back of a tangle of fair hair, before her own hand was grasped. She looked into smiling, friendly very blue eyes.

"Great you've come," June continued. "There's so much work we hardly know how to cope. Mo and I are run off our feet. None of our boats are properly manned, but it'll be easier now there are more of us."

June's warmth and clear message that she was needed dispelled any misgivings Catherine might have had. Her spirits, never low for long, lifted. June walked with Catherine back up the path, explaining the situation.

"At the moment there are four crews. Each is supposed to have a coxswain in charge, usually a leading wren, a stoker and a deckhand. Two crews at a time are on duty for twenty four hours, running noon to noon. We are so short handed we've had to run the boats with just a coxswain and only one crew, either a stoker or a deckhand. There aren't many trained wren stokers which doesn't help."

They emerged from the tow-path and turned right into a lane. June continued.

"Deckhands have to cover for Cox's when they're on leave and no one can ever go off sick." She squeezed Catherine's arm. "Great you've come."

This was the early summer of 1943 and the country had been at war for nearly four years. The Allies were on the advance in the Middle East, working their way towards the toe of Italy. The Germans were about to launch a new offensive on Soviet soil and there were nightly bombing raids on both sides of the channel. The Navy, Army and Air Force were training in unison to prepare for the eventual invasion of Europe. Combined Operational Bases had begun to build up their resources, which meant an increase of landing craft with the attendant support services. H.M.S. Cormorant was one of these establishments. The request for more sea going wrens together with other personnel was linked to the building of strength for the European Offensive.

June led Catherine into a small, detached house, surrounded by rough grass which might once have been a lawn. "This is Pantiles, undoubtedly a pre-war des. res. but for us Wrens to live in for the duration."

Catherine's allotted bunk was on the ground floor in what must have been a sitting room with French windows opening onto a tangled shrubbery. The bunk above Catherine's was already occupied. June, standing by the door, called out introductions.

"Liz, this is Catherine, just arrived. Catherine this is Liz Howard, straight off a stoker's course and got here this morning. I'll be back to scoop you both up before supper and take you across to where we mess."

June was gone, leaving the newcomers together.

Later, Catherine could never remember if her first impression of Liz had been her appearance or her sophisticated manner. The first thought that came to mind was how incongruous for such a glamorous person to become a stoker, dealing most of the time with dirty engines. But Liz Howard loved engines almost as much as she cared for clothes and was meticulous in her care of each.

Liz eased herself into a sitting position and dangled her long legs, sheathed luxuriously in black silk stockings, over the side of the bunk. Catherine noted her slender wrists and ankles and wished her own hair was longer and curled at the ends.

"You O.K. with sleeping underneath? I don't mind taking it in turns."

Liz pushed her hair back from her face and looked hard at Catherine.

"What d'you think of this place? It's a bit off the beaten track. God knows how we get to any bright lights. Wonder what one does off duty. Where've you come from?"

Liz paused for breath and Catherine rushed in a reply. She wanted to appear confident but felt like a junior at school in the presence of a sixth former. She was too taken up with her own feelings of inadequacy to notice Liz was covering up her own shyness with chatter.

Catherine unpacked her few belongings and was comforted by the familiar sight of her family in the travelling photograph frame. She placed it carefully on the top of her shared chest of drawers.

Liz was interested. "Are those your parents? You're lucky to have two brothers and a sister. I'm on my own. Where do you come in the pecking order?"

"Helen's two years older than me, she's a nurse and Alec's only fifteen and still at school."

Catherine liked talking about them.

"Sam's the same age as Helen, but he's my cousin. He lives with us as his parents are dead. Are those your parents?"

She pointed to a silver framed photograph of a pretty dark haired woman, like Liz but older, standing by a man in military uniform.

"That's them. At least it was my father; he was killed in action last year."

Liz did not elaborate. Catherine was uncertain what to say. Just to be sorry did not sound good enough. But Liz did not appear to expect a reply and hurried on.

"My mother's working for a Government Department in London. I don't see much of her but my Grandparents are great and I go to them when I can. They don't live far from here."

She felt in her shoulder bag and pulled out a snap-shot of an elderly couple sitting on a garden seat with two spaniels lying at their feet.

"The smaller one is Tess, she's mine. I'd love to have her here but it's probably not allowed and anyway she's really better off with them."

Catherine admired the speckled spaniel with her tongue hanging out. She felt more at ease as she continued to unpack. June found them chatting away comfortably when she returned to take them to supper.

The Mess where the Wrens ate had been the dining room of a large, impressive, white pillared house. It housed the W.R.N.S. Administration and accommodated most of the Wren Officers. The White House, as it was known, was next door to the Naval Shore Base, a large complex of corrugated huts sprinkled with two storey brick buildings. The sentry at the gate and the White Ensign signified that this was H.M.S. Cormorant.

The atmosphere in the Mess seemed to Catherine, relaxed and informal. They helped themselves to food at the serving hatch through which she could see a large kitchen, known as the galley. Girls in overalls, wreathed in steam, produced a constant supply of food. There was a continual hum of conversation and stream of people hurrying to get fed before either going on watch or off from duty.

"Oh dear, toad in the hole yet again," June remarked.

"More hole than toad," a girl across the table grumbled sleepily.

Catherine wondered if she had just woken up.

"Still on nights?" June asked.

The girl yawned and nodded.

"Jenny's in the signals office up at Base," June explained.

"Must dash and change, or I'll be late getting on watch."

Jenny looked at the clock on the wall and began to bolt her supper.

"Real stodge, this spotted dick, reminds me of school," Liz remarked cheerfully, but she was hungry. "Going for a second?"

Catherine followed her back to the hatch, hoping that the pudding had not run out.

"You'll be even more hungry tomorrow when you've been working," June warned. "Hi Mo, you're up late. Did they keep your food?"

Catherine turned as the small, red haired girl, she had seen on the river, came into the room. She was a real carroty red head and her face was covered in so many freckles they merged into each other.

"Blimey, I could eat a horse."

Mo came across rubbing her hands on the seat of her trousers before shaking hands with Liz and Catherine.

"Which of you is Catherine? You'll be joining me tomorrow, thank the

Lord."

Mo was a Londoner and proud of having been born within the sound of Bow bells. She did not give Catherine a chance to reply.

"It's been a real sod getting those Craft sorted. Number One of five three two is a fussy old woman, he wouldn't let any one ashore till everything was tickety blue."

Her eyes widened and she pursed her lips in disapproval.

"And did you see Bill Owen make his entrance tonight? Made an absolute balls of getting into position. He damn nearly had five thirty on the mud and with a falling tide."

She fetched a covered plate from the hatch and sat down with them.

Catherine noticed the room had begun to empty. They stayed on, watching Mo satisfy her hunger. In between mouthfuls she amused them with the events of her day. Catherine was struck by Mo and June's easy familiarity towards herself and Liz, different to the more authoritative approach from the coxswains towards their crews which she had experienced before. The wren stewards cleared round them and began to lay up the long tables for breakfast.

"Who will you be crewing for?" Catherine asked of Liz as they emerged from the White House into the dusk.

"She's joining me in the Crash boat." June answered for her. "Real luxury to have a qualified stoker on board. The Crash boat's twin diesels are hell to start in the morning."

"Really!" Liz was instantly interested and plied June with questions. Catherine noticed Liz had quite lost her languid look in her enthusiasm for the temperamental diesels.

June handed round cigarettes and the four smoked companionably as she and Mo gave their new crews instructions for the morning before turning in. They were quartered at Russets further down the road. Catherine could hear their footsteps and Mo's voice fading as they merged into the shadows of the tree lined road. She stood for a moment enjoying the night scent of grass and flowers mingled with the more pungent smell of river mud now exposed by the low tide.

"Heavens I'm tired," yawned Liz, "best get our heads down before the grand awakening."

Catherine nodded, suddenly aware of her extreme weariness. Linking arms spontaneously, they crossed the grass to their new home. A Wren

Petty Officer was waiting for them at the front door, tricorn hat under her arm.

"You must be the new boatscrew wrens, Howard and Tenant," she said smiling at them. "Don't forget to sign in; the book's on the table in the kitchen." She inserted herself with care through the blackout curtains which she lifted for them to follow. "Mustn't infringe the blackout regulations."

There was a gossiping group round the table in the kitchen, enjoying a late mug of cocoa. Someone pulled out a couple of stools for them. But the day had been long enough for Catherine and Liz, even a hard bunk was more attractive.

<u>Chapter Two</u>

"There's a letter for you," Catherine called down.

Mo recognised the familiar long blue envelope and knew it to be covered with her mother's spidery writing.

"Thanks for bringing the mail. Did your bike arrive in one piece?"

Catherine's bicycle had at last come from her previous Base, after more than a month's delay. Pantiles was a third of a mile from the Yard, wheels saved time to give extra minutes in bed and helped in collecting mail between trips.

"Watch the foredeck, just scrubbed," Mo warned as Catherine clambered down. The boat sparkled in the late afternoon light, evidence of their earlier efforts. "Ten minutes to our next trip, so let's see what's new."

She slit open the blue envelope using the knife at the end of her lanyard. Catherine nodded and curled up in the bows content to read her own letter.

Darling Mo, I'm writing from the shelter, not much has happened here........Mo's mother wrote of Grandad's allotment and Tom's latest prank as if they were the only events in her life. But Mo, reading between the lines, heard the nightly wail of the warning siren as her mother and five year old brother made their way to the underground at the Angel. She knew her Grandfather would obstinately remain in the narrow terraced house, proof against her mother's persuasion. She pictured war torn streets, the corner shop, which had suffered a near miss, with Mrs Bailey all the while calmly knitting balaclavas for the arctic convoys and her small indomitable mother at the centre of it all. She felt the old compassionate ache, a legacy from her childhood when her father, full of drink, exploded over the threshold disrupting all semblance of happy family life. She folded the letter back in the envelope and sighed. Catherine stuffed her own letter into her pocket and turned enquiringly.

"I wish," said Mo emphatically, "Mum didn't have to stay with Grandad in London. Tom oughtn't to be there either but Mum won't hear of him being evacuated after everything Gina and I went through".

Catherine had already heard something of the Baker sisters' ordeal when they were sent to a Welsh village at the start of the war. The two middle-aged spinsters, allotted as carers, were Chapel and their notions of bringing up children came from their own harsh experiences. Gina had turned to Mo, her elder, for comfort but there was no one for Mo. Rebellion had been the natural outcome.

"Couldn't your Grandad go with them?"

"Obstinate old cuss, he'll only leave feet first," Mo replied crossly. "Here come our passengers," she said, changing the subject as a group of sailors advanced down the narrow Pier, carrying boxes of stores.

The Cutter filled with men returning to their ships. Mo started the engine and Catherine, standing in the bows, cast off the forward line. She made her way past the passengers, to the stern where Mo was at the tiller. Small Mo had to stand on a box to see over the Cutter's bows. She eased the Cutter away from the Pier, nodding at Catherine to open up the Ford V 8 engine, which coughed uncertainly before settling, at full throttle into a throaty song. The boat thrust purposefully through the water travelling towards the flotilla of Landing Craft moored higher up river.

Mo, in charge, absorbed the familiar busy scene. So much going on everywhere from on board the Landing craft to the Maintenance Yard slipways and the hum of machinery coming from the massive boat sheds. It was easy to shrug off troubled thoughts of home and concentrate just on the world about her. She enjoyed the light touch of sun and summer breeze on her face and bare arms as she listened to Catherine's badinage with their passengers. She had settled in so quickly as her crew and friend.

"Tide's turned."

Catherine noted the swing of the smaller moored craft either side of the river.

"Now it's springs it'll be dead low and smellier than ever for late duty trips."

She wrinkled her nose in anticipation.

They left a few men on the catamarans, the water-side approach to the village on the far side of the river. They were in a hurry to quench their thirst at the Duck and Feather.

"Don't enjoy yourselves so much that you miss the last boat," Mo shouted after them. "Bear off for'ard." This was directed to Catherine wielding a boathook in the bows.

"It's a date! Keep us a place. We'll drink to that, Carrots."

Their amused voices followed the duty boat as it continued down river.

It was after six and the slipways were quiet. The second duty Cutter was plying back and forth between the Pier-head and the lower line of Craft, busy collecting men wishing to spend the evening ashore.

"If we tear up for an early supper, there'll be time for a quick cuppa' on 727 before the evening trips start," Mo proposed.

Catherine guessed Dick, one of the men in Mo's life, was responsible for the invitation.

Catherine frowned as she shut off the engine.

"It's running a bit hot and I think it misses a beat sometimes."

She looked round at Mo.

"Hope it doesn't pack up on us. If Liz was around I'd ask her to take a look."

But Liz and June were away in the Crash boat, collecting some officers from the Island.

"Oh heck, looks as if we're needed again already." Mo was gazing up at the Pier-head Quartermaster standing by his hut, waving a large envelope.

"I'd better nip up and see what he wants."

The falling tide had exposed the first slime covered steps and Mo trod carefully before taking the top, dry ones two at a time. Stripey, the three badge Quartermaster was agitated. He quoted his own manager the Boatswain.

"He's sorry, but the signal has got to get to them fast, see and they're lying off Calshot waiting for orders. Crash boat would be best but June's not back yet."

He flapped the brown envelope at Mo.

"One thing, you should have time before your next duty trip."

"Can do, don't worry, Stripey. Tell me where they're lying and we'll be off."

Reassured by her quick response he showed, on the hut's wall chart, where the ship should be.

"Ask the other duty bods, when they go up, to put our supper on one side in case we're late." If we make it at all, she thought prophetically.

"Change of plan," she told Catherine laconically. "Better shove on something warm, it'll be breezy out there."

They shrugged into their seaman's sweaters and Catherine found some chocolate, donated by visiting Americans.

"And I didn't have to give any favours," she grinned and Mo perfectly understood.

As they set course for the entrance of the river, Mo noticed a small motor launch ahead. It was not one she recognised.

It was late August but evenings were already cooler, a warning that summer was running out. Winter was a hard time on the boats when seamanship was tested to the full by wind and heavy weather. Mo was prone to sea sickness which was an added hazard for her. The falling tide ran strongly, helping them on the way. Breakwaters to the east were already exposed, sticking out of the water like old teeth but the shingle bank, forming the spit on the western side of the river was not yet visible. The mournful clang of the marker buoy came over as a salutary warning to keep clear.

Catherine shouted to Mo, above the noise of the engine. "Just look at that boat! Aren't they too far over?"

"Mm, they may draw less water than us."

Mo was concentrating on keeping in the channel. Then it happened. The small motor boat was suddenly no longer moving. Its engine roared as the Coxswain slammed the gear into reverse, with no effect. They were stuck fast. The tide was in full ebb and the shingle bank would not yield.

Mo slowed down but knew any attempt to tow them off would be foolhardy. A wildly gesticulating figure emerged from the cabin, three broad gold bands visible on his waving arms.

"Cripes, it's Commander Jackson! There'll be trouble."

The Commander of the neighbouring Base on the upper reaches of the river was renowned for his short temper. His angry voice demanded to be rescued, instantly.

"Suppose we'll have to try," Mo sighed. "I'll just put our nose in and he'll have to paddle to get on board".

She inched the Cutter towards the shallow water while Catherine eased the engine's throttle. The Commander was silent, watching, preparing to jump.

He suddenly yelled, "You'll have to come closer than that".

Catherine heard Mo muttering under her breath, "No bloody fear".

The bows of the Cutter crunched and the deflated Commander slopped across and clambered aboard.

"Hard astern and rev up."

Mo swiftly gave the order. Catherine obediently slipped the gear into position and opened the throttle. The engine coughed twice and died. She tried, despairingly, to coax the V 8 to life. It was obstinately silent. The motor launch had company.

Commander Jackson was speechless. Perhaps as well, when a near tearful Catherine truthfully but unwisely said, "It's no good, I haven't a clue what's wrong with the beastly thing."

His face was the colour of a ripe tomato and Catherine hoped he did not have a heart condition. Just at that moment the Crash boat rounded the point and foamed into the river. June recognising the double disaster, calmly and efficiently handled first her boat into a rescue position and then took on the irate Commander. Catherine felt it was a pleasure to hand him over. At the same time, June accepted the delivery of the Boatswain's brown envelope.

"Try cleaning the weed-trap, or perhaps your plugs are dirty," Liz advised Catherine as she flirted with the purring twin diesels on board the Crash boat. She politely but firmly told Commander Jenson where he should sit and, slightly condescendingly, helped him empty his shoes, which he had forgotten to remove before paddling. June was amused, knowing that Liz expected engines and passengers to do her bidding, which they invariably did.

"Sleep well!" the rescuers called as they sped away to deliver the cargo before returning to sort out the beached Cutter's late trips.

It was a golden rule to remain with one's boat under all circumstances. Mo and Catherine had no option but to stay with the Cutter. It would be the best part of the night before they floated off.

"But at least we've got company," Mo consoled Catherine, peering bleakly into the engine.

The decks of the motor launch were aslant but as the water fell two sailors jumped down and scrunched across the shingle to the Cutter.

"In trouble then?"

Catherine sighed with relief when she noticed the stocky, curly haired lad's stoker badge, as he immediately rolled up his sleeves and knowledgeably, felt about in the dead engine.

"Leave it to Stokes, he's a whiz with engines."

Taff, the Cox, was dark and wirey, the taller of the two.

"Reckon it'll be early morning before we get off. Likely to be cold too."

A sneaky wind had sprung up as daylight faded. Mo walked with Taff along the shingle bank. They stared out over the mud flats, glistening in the half-light. The mocking clang of the marker buoy mingled with soft bird noises from the marshy fringe of the river. It was desolate and she shivered.

Stokes finished cleaning the plugs and checked the V 8 carefully.

"Reckon she'll run sweet now," he said, wiping his hands on the cotton waste handed to him by Catherine. She had cleaned the weed-trap and felt better.

The four of them huddled down in the stern of the Cutter, where the half canopy would protect them from the rising wind. They draped the sailors duffle coats round their shoulders and shared round a pack of hard tack biscuits.

"They're so dry they stick in my throat," Catherine complained.

Stokes felt for his tin of tobacco and cigarette papers.

"Ticklers all round?" he suggested and expertly rolled four very thin cigarettes, allowing the girls to lick and seal their own. The tobacco was harsh and stung Catherine's mouth but she did not say anything because Stokes had been so kind.

The night was dark. The warmth under the lumped coats from close bodies was comforting. Mo sensed that Catherine slept. Stokes, too, became quiet. Taff talked quietly; his Welsh voice rising and falling rhythmically. His home was in the Rhonda Valley.

"Men in my family expect to go down the mines, automatic like, but I'll never go back to that. The sea's for me now."

"Even sticking on a shingle bank?" Mo teased him. She told him about her bad time in Wales, with Miss Ada and Miss Maud.

"I know about Chapel folk," Taff laughed. Then startled her by confiding, "I'm a married man, you know".

Mo was amazed. He seemed no older than herself and she did not at all wish to be tied to one person, have babies and suffer her Mum's dreary life. But Taff was in love and did not want to be free. After a while he became quiet and Mo was the last one awake, listening to the night sounds and wondering if Dick missed her.

Mo woke suddenly. Catherine's hand was on her arm. Water sucked and gurgled round the Cutter's stern. She was stiff and cramped and woke the still sleeping men for them to get back to their own boat. They waved as they crossed, just dry-shod and climbed aboard. The wind was lively but the dark sky held that mellow light preceding dawn.

They waited while water rose, like searching fingers over the bank, up and around them. Everywhere they looked seemed covered in water but they were still not afloat. Then with a series of bumps they were free.

Catherine crossed her fingers and pressed the starter. One groan and the engine sang into life.

"Thank you God for Stokes," Catherine prayed as she and Mo waved to the launch. They would soon be off too.

The sky to the East was pearly grey, when they finally secured the Cutter. The Quartermaster gave them mugs of thick, scalding tea from the pot slowly stewing on the top of the stove in his hut. "727 sent this ashore for you." He handed Mo an envelope, smaller than the one he had waved earlier.

"Catherine, Dick's got a stand easy and has booked the Whaler. Would you like to come for a sail when we come off duty?" she enquired. But Catherine had a date of her own.

Chapter Three

"Gosh, I'm hot, and fed up with pumping. I only hope it's not a puncture. It seems to need an awful lot of air." Catherine had hung her jacket over the handlebars and spoke in jerks between pumps.

"When we get there, old Will, down at the bridge can take a look. If it pegs out before, we'll cadge a lift. Must get going as Gran will be expecting us. If we're late, she'll have us raped or under a lorry."

Liz hitched her gas mask across her shoulders and wheeled her bicycle with a bulging saddle bag into the lane. Catherine crammed her rolled up pyjamas into her own front basket and followed.

They pedalled down the lane, past the entrance of the Yard, guarded by the sentry and turned right, away from the river. Once out of the village the air smelled fresh and flowery from hedges still heavy with summer growth. Fully clothed trees stood guardians of golden fields of stubble, left from the harvest.

"It feels I'm on holiday, leaving the boats." Catherine felt curiously free.

"Mo and Dick won't get far in the Whaler with so little wind."

"They might get further than you think."

Liz raised her eyebrows. "Is Dick fond of her?"

"She doesn't say much. He's always trying to date her, but he's only one of lots."

"Maybe it's safety in numbers. I'd better go first here; it's a bit narrow." Liz cycled ahead.

The lane ran between steep banks and cycling single file made it difficult to talk. Liz's mind ran ahead in anticipation of their arrival. She wanted everything to be the same, for them to look no older and nothing wrong with the dogs. A gnawing anxiety had been with her, since her father had been killed in North Africa, nine months earlier. He'd gone without a goodbye yet he was supposed to love her, his only child. The one person in the world she could talk to was no longer. She could not tell him she was a qualified stoker and made engines work, nor of the boats and her new friends. He wasn't there for her, not anywhere. Her anger rose sickeningly.

Could someone so real disappear into nothing? The fear was that if she did not talk about him she might forget. She could not upset her grandparents; after all he was their child, and her mother was always busy or away. Free wheeling down hill, with wind on her face and in her hair she was exhilarated. Liz pushed the sad thoughts away and began to enjoy the ride.

Catherine caught up and stayed, the road was wider. Her short brown hair stood up in spikes, framing her heart shaped face.

"Whew! That down bit was great. I really needed that wind to cool me. Funny how you feel wind but can't see it."

Liz was silent. She stored Catherine's wind remark away, to think on later.

"If we could ever manage a forty eight hour pass I'd love you to come to my home." Catherine added uncertainly, "that's if you'd like to". She was horribly conscious of the two years between them and was flattered Liz sought her company.

"That's a super idea," Liz replied promptly. This left Catherine wondering how it would really work out. Her mother could be tricky but her father would tease Liz, in a kind way, which was probably what she missed without a dad.

"I'd like you to meet my cousin Sam. He wanted to fly but was turned down because of his handicap so he's staying at College."

"Why? What's wrong with him?" Liz was interested.

"Well, you see he was in that beastly car accident which killed his parents. He broke his legs really badly and one's now a bit shorter than the other. Usually he's pretty cheerful but I think he minds not being in the forces."

"You're so lucky having a brother, sister and cousin around. Big families must be fun. Do you know June has four brothers and sisters and they live on a farm?" Liz braked violently as a cat streaked across her front wheel.

Catherine wrenched at her handlebars to avoid collision and ended up in the ditch.

"Ouch I'm on stinging nettles!" she squealed. "Blast that suicidal animal, my tyre's really flat now."

There was no sign of the cat.

"Must have lost one of its nine lives."

Liz found a dock leaf and they gloomily surveyed the injured bike. "The Fox and Hounds should be near with a telephone. Shall I go on and get help?"

Catherine followed slowly, pushing the crippled bike. She heard a vehicle behind, coming up fast and flattened herself close to the hedge. Brakes screamed and a huge man in American uniform bent over the side of an open jeep.

"Hi Doll, you in trouble? Hank's the name. Guess you could easy persuade me for a ride."

Catherine thought the small forage cap looked absurd perched on his closely cropped head. His cauliflower ears were like a boxer's but his velvety brown eyes twinkled. She was hot and tired and hoped her uniform was proof against any grandmotherly fears.

They caught up with Liz before the Fox and Hounds and Hank scooped her complete with bicycle aboard, without flexing a muscle. He then made short work of the four miles to Bridge End while Catherine and Liz clung to each other and the seats, concentrating on survival as they hoped Hank, the demon driver was on the road.

"Swell meeting you dames, this O.K.?" he drawled as he jammed on his brakes and the jeep slammed to a stop. As soon as they, with bicycles, were on the ground, Hank was off with noisy acceleration, jaws still working.

"Do they chew in their sleep?" Catherine questioned.

"What you doing with them Yanks?"

Old Will at the garage, with its single pump and empty forecourt, was disapproving. He sucked his teeth at the flat tyre.

"Leave it out the back. She'll be ready come morning."

Catherine left her bicycle propped in the cluttered backyard.

"You're an old angel." Liz blew him a kiss and treated him to a melting smile.

Will softened, "Go on with you Missy".

Her basket strapped to the handlebars, Catherine perched on the saddle and dangled her feet clear of the pedals.

"Hang on, here we go."

Liz stood on the pedals and steered an erratic course away from the garage.

"Wouldn't like to do this for long, you weigh a ton."

The iron gates had long been taken towards the war effort but stone pillars with crouching lions marked the entrance. The top-heavy machine careered unsteadily through the opening and carried on down a drive, flanked by rhododendrons. A twist and they were in front of an old house, Georgian windows peering out of a curtain of gnarled wisteria.

"Darling, darling Liz, how lovely you're here. And is this Catherine?"

Liz sighed, she was in her grandmother's arms, smelling a mix of soap and lavender. Her grandfather stood by sucking his empty pipe and the spaniels wagged in welcome. Nothing had changed.

'This is Liz's photograph,' Catherine thought, 'only I'm in it too'.

After tea, seed-cake a speciality of the house, Liz and Colonel Howard, her grandfather, showed Catherine round the garden. The spaniels ran here and there, hurrying them along. Shrubbery and rose garden were still intact but the rest of the originally formal plan had been planted with vegetables, digging for victory as urged by Churchill. Chickens scratched busily on the grass tennis court.

"Rhode island reds, not bad layers. Have to shut 'em up at night or they'd be a meal for mister Reynard. Cunning devils these foxes."

The Colonel's white moustache bristled; he was enjoying showing Catherine around.

They ate supper in the big kitchen while the dogs snoozed in their basket by the stove. Catherine noticed that Alice Howard, the Colonels wife, had tired lines round her eyes but she served up roast chicken and blackberry pie for her guests. Was it one of the Rhode islands? They sat on as dusk gathered, unwilling to draw the blackout and switch on lights.

"The Yanks have taken over St Ann's and the girls have gone to Devon," the Colonel told Liz.

"It's a big girls' school near here, used to be very swanky," Liz explained. "Oh, I wonder if your rescuing Hank was on his way there."

"We've agreed to put some of the officers up here. After all we've room enough and they'll eat at the school."

"Long as they don't pinch my room," Liz said with a mouthful of fruit pie. "I'd hate that."

"My dear Liz your room is sacrosanct. Your grandmother won't let anyone else use it, not even your mother when she comes, which isn't often; she's so busy with that work in Town. Not sure what it's all about, probably hush-hush."

Liz frowned. "She writes but doesn't say anything about her work. She seems to meet lots of people."

Alice Howard looked across at her granddaughter. "Perhaps that's a good thing, darling. She could be so lonely otherwise."

She turned to Catherine, changing the subject. "Liz says you live in Brighton. We used to stay there before the war, dreadful pebbly beach but I liked the West Pier."

"The sea front is all shut off with barbed wire barriers and the beach is mined."

Catherine noticed the Colonel had casually put his arm round Liz's shoulder and her face had cleared.

The nine o'clock news on the wireless was all about Italy.

"Reckon they're on the point of collapse but it'll be a stiff fight with Gerry up the leg."

The Colonel showed them his stickers on a wall map marking the Allies position.

"Next move should be an offensive into Europe, you girls would know something of that, but less said the better, careless talk costs lives."

Catherine and Liz thought of the Landing Craft back on the river and shared a smile.

Liz's bedroom was over the porch, shaded by fronds of wisteria. A second bed had been made up for Catherine. She climbed into the cold, linen sheets, much softer than the coarse ones at Pantiles. She was pleased to be with Liz, the house was large and unfamiliar.

Liz turned out the light and drew back the heavy curtains to open the window. Wind stirred in the trees near the house. A dog barked or was it a fox, some way off. She climbed into bed, happy to be home. Catherine's remark, on the ride over, surfaced in her mind.

"You know you said something about wind being felt but not seen. D'you think it could be the same for people?"

Catherine could not see her friend's face but she heard the strain in her voice.

"There has to be lots we don't know," she said carefully. "Feeling but not seeing wind might be a clue." She sat up and leaned towards the dark shape in the other bed. "It's about your father isn't it?"

"I can't get any feel of him. He doesn't seem to be anywhere. It's awful." Liz was despairing. "There's nothing left of him to hang onto. He died in the desert so I can't even see his grave. It feels as if he never was."

The words hung in the darkness, drenched in sadness. Catherine wanted to help her friend so much.

"Life's a funny business." She corrected herself, "I mean funny peculiar not ha-ha. Sometimes it goes wrong for me if I try too hard".

She thought of the time when her own father had been hurt fire fighting in the City.

"When I've had a shock I go sort of numb and I can't really feel. Maybe you're still shocked and have to wait a bit to feel."

Catherine looked across at the hunched figure. "You know you're still part of your Dad and your Gran and Grandpa are too; you could talk to them."

"I could try. Suppose they might be numb too and finding it difficult. I can't talk to my mother at all." Liz came back through the darkness.

"Well I wouldn't be able to talk to mine either".

Liz laughed at Catherine's definite statement. The tension broke and they drifted off to sleep.

The morning was grey with a hint of rain. The Colonel had walked the dogs to fetch Catherine's bicycle. Liz was packing her saddle-bag when her grandmother appeared clutching a jar of bramble jelly and a stack of ginger bread.

"Just room for these." She was hopeful. "And look, I found this snap of your father, when he was about your age. Would you like it?" She reached out and gave Liz a hug. They clung for a moment sharing their grief.

"Ride carefully. Come again soon," the Colonel shouted them away with Tess, the younger spaniel, straining to follow.

"Heavens, look at the time! We'll have to keep going or we'll be late on duty."

"It's been super. Your grandparents are lovely." Catherine put on speed. "I feel as if I've been away ages."

Chapter Four

The weather changed and the lazy days of the Indian summer were a memory as the equinoctial gales swept in. The wind stirring the tops of the conifers outside Russets reminded June of wind in the Elms on the Farm and her father shouting for the ricks to be covered before a storm. It was a relief not to be there, expected to jump to his demands. How was the land-girl coping and how did her mother put up with him?

The curtains billowed into the room, knocking a hairbrush off the top of a chest of drawers. A body in a bunk moaned in protest and burrowed back to sleep.

"Are you awake?"

Mo's coppery head appeared round the door.

"Looks as if we're in for a stormy watch."

Mo was dressed with her bundled oilskins under her arm.

"Shan't be a jiffy," June whispered back, careful not to wake the sleepers. She struggled into her trousers and flung on shirt and seaman's sweater. Straightening her bunk and smoothing the woven anchor bedspread over the lumps, took minutes.

Mo waited by their bicycles where the lane was sheltered but as soon as they turned down the tow path they felt the stinging rain.

"Got your pills?"

June knew Mo was a bad sailor in rough weather. Mo patted her jacket pocket.

"Looks as if we're in for a blow."

The sentry on the gate to the yard emerged from his shelter as they panted through.

"O.K. for some, snug in his little hut," Mo complained, queasy at the thought of it. "At least it'll be reasonable on the river and I've got mostly duty trips before I'm off at noon. Any idea what's in store for you?"

"Could be Cowes."

The Crash boat, built for speed, collected long trips which would take them out of the sheltering river.

Catherine and Liz waited at the Pier-head in their oilskins and Catherine's serious face looked out from under a sou'wester.

"You look like an ad for skipper's sardines," Mo laughed and Catherine flushed.

June added quickly, "You're the wise one, just look at that black sky. Bet we'll all wish we'd been as prepared when that hits us".

The Cutter left first, bound for the Yard, to collect a maintenance party. Catherine coiled the bow line neatly on the fore-deck. She reminded June of her young sister Patty, keen to do the right thing but credulous and lacking confidence, needing to grow up. The river scene in the early light was drab and vaguely menacing. Tiny curling waves slapped petulantly at moored Craft. The disturbed surface of the river reflected the leaden sky, merging land and water in one great grey wash of colour.

Liz wiped her hands on an oily rag.

"O.K. for you to start up," she advised and June went forward to the controls on the right in the wheel-house. The twin engines roared into life. June grinned approval, over the din.

"Ahoy there! Are you the folks taking me across to Cowes?"

June recognised Pete Durant, one of the signals officers from Cormorant. She nodded and he jumped down into the boat.

"Cast off and bear off," she shouted out to Liz, waiting on the fore deck. Once clear of the Pier, Liz stowed the boat hook below, mindful that decks would be awash once out of the river.

"Pete's delivering sailing orders to a tank landing craft that's lying in Cowes," June explained as she set course for the mouth of the river.

"Glad I am it's the Crash boat and not one of your Cutters, at least the ride will be dry." Pete removed his cap. "How does your launch ride in a rough sea?"

"She's not bad heading into it, but needs watching when it's a following sea. I have to keep her out of troughs or she's inclined to dive." June said this so lightly that Liz wondered if she was serious. Pete made no comment.

A strong south-west wind hit the boat as it left the sheltering arm of land. The emerging scene was wild. Ragged wave tops showed white against the sombre sky and the sea between was a tumble of dirty green.

June planted her feet firmly on the moving deck and gripped the wheel. She felt the boat rise and shudder as it rocketed over the banked up waves and slapped into the hollows. The boat was alive under her hands like a spirited horse on the edge of bolting. She was in tune, automatically adjusting engine revs to ease the bumpy ride. Liz looked and learned, caught up in June's concentration and the drama.

Pete watched the girls. He was impressed by June's calm confidence. She was in control, gripping the wheel and using the engines to advantage. Strongly built and reliable, fair hair all over the place and a hole in one elbow of her sweater, he had met June before. The other one, Liz, was different, tall and dark, cool and composed, almost like a model. Pete hoped he would become better acquainted.

Close into Cowes, the sea became quieter. The drop in wind and relatively smoother water released some of June's tension. Liz pulled on her oilskin and collecting the boat hook, prepared to come alongside. The harbour was crowded with sheltering craft but there was no sign of an L.C.T.

"Go alongside that M.F.V.," Pete instructed, "I'll nip ashore and try and find out what's happening".

Liz put out the fenders and hung on while Pete scrambled up the steep side of the vessel. He took the lines with him and made the Crash boat secure. There was a sudden silence when June shut off the engines.

"Hullo there, where the hell did you spring from?"

A balding head appeared at one of the portholes, almost on a level with the Crash boat's deck.

"Teas up, like a cup?" the talking head continued. "You're sheltered enough here so leave your boat. She won't go anywhere. Come and meet the lads."

The smoky cabin of the sturdy Fleet following vessel was full of elderly men, mostly called back from retirement.

"Who have you got there, James? A couple of waifs blown in from the storm?" A tall, silver haired man handed Liz an off white towel to dry her hair. "Not much of a hand with laundry, don't you know," he apologised.

The tea was thick and strong and went well with bread and jam doorsteps. Blue liners, duty free cigarettes, were passed round and added to the warm fug. Pete's footsteps sounded on deck and his anxious face appeared at the top of the companionway.

"The perishing L.C.T.'s not here. They're apparently conducting some sort of trials at sea." Pete was worried. "We must find her to give her these orders and take off the technicians who are only on board for the trials. They will have to come back to the river with us." He frowned. "Afraid you'll be late off watch by the time we've chased the damned ship half way round the Solent or maybe further."

The elderly lads waved them off and James shouted after Liz, "Give my best to the Colonel. He'll remember that clapped out thirty five footer he towed into Folkestone". Liz remembered her grandfather had used his old yacht in the evacuation of Dunkirk. It was a strange coincidence, learned over tea that James had shared in the experience.

June knew when they left Cowes, they were in for a really rough ride. Wind against tide had built up into an increasingly troubled sea. The Crash boat developed an extremely uncomfortable motion. Pete directed June westwards down the Solent towards Hurst Castle and the Needles. Heading directly into the heavy weather, he remained in the cockpit, anxiously scanning the horizon for the missing ship.

Eventually she was seen, a long way ahead, a grey shape moving off Yarmouth. June sighed with relief. Navigating the narrow passage, off Hurst, with such wind against tide would have been horrendous.

Pete verified the numbers on the ship's stern. Binoculars were trained on them from the bridge and Pete waved his arms indicating he must board.

"Go as close as you can and I'll jump," Pete told June. "Liz, stay below. It's too rough to attempt to hitch on to this tin beast." He crouched on the fore deck, clinging onto the cabin combing as June slowly approached the cumbersome Craft. She could see Pete's legs through the blurred windscreen.

The Crash boat crept forward towards the towering side of the L.C.T. A wave caught and carried them high above the monster's deck. As they came down, June glimpsed Pete's flying legs and then he was aboard the beast. She opened both throttles full and the Crash boat spun out of reach of the punishing metal.

"He got a drenching but he made it." Liz laughed as they lay off waiting for the next move.

Someone shouted through a megaphone. June throttled down and Liz went to the stern to listen. "It sounds as if they're going to turn into the weather to give us protection alongside."

June was sceptical but watched the cumbersome Craft slowly change position. A second message from the megaphone and June took her own boat in again, biting her lips in concentration. A touch ahead with the starboard engine, port into neutral, a touch astern and they were there. Some one flung a line, Liz, poised on the bows, scrabbled for the wet rope, grasped it and took a swift turn round a cleat. The combined strength of the wind and sea was too much and Liz was left, only, with the frayed end. June had to veer away to protect themselves from the metal sides of the Landing Craft.

"For heaven's sake come back down here," she snapped, concerned for Liz' safety on the slippery deck. "Can't they see they'll have to jump, like Pete?" She was angry. "It could take an age if there are many to come. I hope we've got enough fuel, we're a long way from home."

"That's no worry." Liz was reassuring and June felt better that she was once more down below.

Another shout from the megaphone and a small group appeared on deck.

"Get ready for an invasion," Liz grinned.

June prepared for the pick up. The first time, two men leapt and dropped safely onto the foredeck and a third slithered into the stern. They crowded wet and laughing into the cabin.

"Three down, two to go and one will be your Flags. Good grief you're girls."

A damp Petty Officer was astonished.

"From the tin can, we took you for sailors."

Pete and the fourth engineer in the party landed without mishap. The truant L.C.T. gave a farewell salute on her siren and set sail purposely for the westerly entrance of the Solent. June shrugged away tiredness and turned the laden Crash boat for home.

One engineer had torn trousers and a gashed leg, landing badly and another had lost all his brace buttons. The Crash boat's regulation First Aid kit came in for the casualty but Liz ran out of safety pins for the braces repair. In the end a piece of cod-line did as well. Everyone was wet and cold but a flask of warming brandy did the rounds and there was relieved laughter and chat.

June felt remote. She and the boat were alone in an endless sea of trouble. It was important to maintain speed and stay ahead of the, now, following sea to avoid waves toppling in the stern and pooping the boat. At the same time she had to balance the boat and counteract its tendency to dive.

"Shall I tell your passengers to settle towards the stern? That should act as a kind of ballast."

Pete's suggestion made sense. It felt more stable and then June was aware he had returned to stand beside her. It was not so lonely. By the time they reached the comparative shelter of Southampton Water she had mastered most of her boat's idiosyncrasies. River entrance within sight, she allowed thoughts of food and a hot bath.

"June, the port engine is running rather too warm; not sure what's wrong." Liz caught her attention. "Can you manage on the starboard alone, while I take a look?"

This would cut the speed considerably, but there was no alternative. "Thank God for two engines!" June gave Liz the appropriate reply.

The maintenance team was ready to help but Liz preferred to roll up her sleeves and set to work on her own engine.

"Suppose I can't help?" Pete was hopeful.

"Nice of you to offer, but no thank you," Liz replied firmly. "Just pass that spanner," she requested the Petty Officer Stoker.

The port diesel was ready in time for June to use coming alongside the Pier.

"Thought you'd done a bunk."

The crew of the opposite watch were waiting to take over.

"Leave the boat to us; you must be starving. We'll sort out any problems."

This was a generous offer, not to be refused. June and Liz collected up their wet gear and followed the passengers ashore.

"I'll be in contact. Don't forget I owe you for getting us there and back." Pete was off up the Pier before them all, in a hurry to report to his office.

June and Liz pedalled wearily past the Yard entrance. The Sailor on the gate called out pityingly, "You girls aren't 'alf late going off watch. What kept you?"

"The weather delayed us a bit," June smiled at the understatement.

Liz pointed to a watery sun, hesitating through a rift in the clouds.

"Typical, it's going to clear now we're back on dry land."

Chapter Five

"It's my birthday, and I'm starting a whole new year of life," Catherine reminded her reflection. The face she knew too well stared back. She examined herself critically, nose too long, mouth too large, forehead too low, mousy hair growing up obstinately from a widow's peak and blue eyes on the dark side. She sighed. It was disappointing to be so unremarkable. Better by far to have glamour hair like Liz or red hair like tiny Mo or a natural blond like June. Was there any hope? Could she improve with age like wine and cheese. But cheese sometimes developed whiskers like Great Aunt Mabel who was so uncomfortable to kiss. Catherine chuckled as she turned away from the mirror and missed seeing the transformation into a cheeky urchin.

Today it was more fitting to be Catherine than Wren Tenant, but she had so few civilian clothes. School uniform had been exchanged for a regulation W.R.N.S.' and few clothing coupons over. The blue sweater was fairly new and it went all right with the tweed skirt passed down by Helen.

"Like to borrow my scarf? It would tone in rather well." Liz was considering. The soft silk square made a difference to the outfit. "Have a good time, maybe we'll meet up at the Duck and Feather," she laughed. "That's if you don't get stuck in the woods on the way. June and I are meeting Pete and some friend of his there at seven."

Catherine ran down the lane. She did not want to be early but now she was frightened of being late. Agony, if he wasn't there. Then she saw him coming out of the village stores.

"I thought we could munch these if we get hungry."

Chris gave Catherine the bag of apples and squeezed her arm. "Happy birthday! You look different out of uniform. I'd like to have come out of mine."

Catherine liked him as he was, with the sub-lieutenant's single gold ring on his sleeve. It was strange being with him alone, not the same as meeting on board when Dick and Mo were there.

"Let's have an apple," she said.

She was not hungry but it was a way of breaking the silence. They walked up the lane, munching, leaving the village to the south. Catherine had chosen to visit the woods on the opposite side of the river. She had seen them from the Cutter as mysterious and inviting. A bridge across the higher reaches of the river should take them directly there.

"Funny to think the river is so close; you can't see it at all from here."

Chris took a large bite out of his apple. The river was mostly hidden from view by trees and dense foliage, only once or twice they caught the silvery gleam of water before trees closed in again.

"I love the autumn." Catherine threw the apple core into the hedge for the birds. "It's nearly always lovely weather for my birthday," she waved expansively at the clear blue sky, "which is pretty good considering its right at the end of October."

"That'll be every year of eighteen years?" Chris teased from his superior position of twenty-three. "I can't give my birthdays the same write up, although June ought to be more reliable. I remember it snowing one year when Dad had a hell of a journey across the moors to stitch up some farmer who had been careless with a scythe. But that's Yorkshire for you, when you're lucky to get any summer at all."

"Bronte country." Catherine looked sideways at him, taking in his slight build and fair complexion. Not much like Heathcliff even if my name could be Cathy, she smiled to herself.

"Sounds as if you're a reader. I'm not much of a hand at books, prefer to be doing things." Chris scuffed a stone along the road. "Did you know Cormorant is getting together a mixed hockey team? Said I'd join. How about you?"

"I loved hockey at school, so yes please." Catherine had played in the second eleven.

The lane joined the main road just before the bridge. There was no traffic and Catherine hung over the parapet listening to the watery sound of the flowing river as it sucked at the sides of the bridge.

The hum of approaching transport broke the spell.

"Come on!" Chris urged, pulling Catherine along, across the bridge. "We'll be mown down if we don't watch out."

They reached the safety of the grass verge as the first motorcycle outriders appeared. The long column of armoured cars, trucks and tanks took a while to pass. Soldiers in the back of the trucks waved and called out to Catherine. She smiled and waved back.

"Whew, that was quite a convoy. Weren't some of the soldiers Canadians?"

Chris nodded, "There's bound to be a steady build up of troops from now on." He broke off, "Shouldn't we go over that stile? The path looks as if it could lead to the woods."

The sun shining through dying leaves cast a golden light. Catherine looked up into the high arch of ancient trees. "I feel like I'm in a cathedral."

"Hey, steady there, Johnny head in air." Chris caught her as she tripped over a root. He was suddenly very close. His arms tightened round her and his breath was on her face as he held her steady. She moved away and they walked on in silence.

The stream caught them by surprise, emerging from a mossy bank as a mini waterfall. The water plopped into a shallow bed that wound this way and that on a journey to the river. Catherine cried out with pleasure and tested the water with her fingers.

"It is so cold, but what a treasure. There must be a hidden spring in the hillside."

She was entranced at the stream's sparkling clarity and movement.

Chris was equally intrigued. "We get lots of the same at home. More natural there with so much limestone about." He removed his jacket and cap, and rolled up his shirtsleeves. "Shall we see if we can make a pool? There's enough stuff lying around to make a dam."

"What fun, that's a great idea." Catherine pushed up her own sleeves, very willing to help. They gathered twigs, moss and stones and worked like beavers. The water gradually formed a small deep pool. Chris fashioned a piece of bark into a lip which he placed at the centre of the lower bank to encourage water from the pool to fall in a cascade, allowing the stream to continue down to the river.

Work finished, they sank lazily back on the grass, looking at and listening to their creation. Chris divided the last apple. Catherine leaned against him. It seemed a natural progression when she felt his arms round her. He kissed the top of her head and she turned easily and naturally to respond. Was this the beginning of making love? Her only experience had been holding hands in the cinema and a furtive goodnight kiss at the front door, always in the dark. It was strange in daylight. She put her arms round Chris and enjoyed the kiss which followed. Then he touched her breasts and she was not sure. Despite having reached eighteen, she felt self- conscious, unable to respond.

Chris sighed, "You are so young Catherine, with an awful lot to learn. I don't think this is the time," he checked himself, "you know you'll need to watch the lads, some are out to get what they can".

He rose to his feet, pulling her up quite roughly. "Better get moving, we've still a long way to go."

Catherine was relieved and put out at the same time. She was curious as to what might have happened next.

"You know I've been out with lots of boys and eighteen's not so young," she defended herself.

"You're gorgeous and I wouldn't swap you with Marta Hari," Chris was reassuring.

"But her legs were fabulous, much better than mine."

"She'd never have looked so good in bell bottoms," he teased. "Come on, forget about the Hari woman's legs, decision time. Which path, up hill or down dale?"

They chose the higher to avoid the reed beds near the river. Unfortunately the path ended abruptly at a high wall. The young saplings in the wood were too slender to climb.

"If I get on your shoulders I might reach that one," Catherine pointed to an adolescent birch close to the wall. "It would be easier if you were taller, as it is," Catherine gasped reaching for the branch, "not sure I can make it".

"Up you go." A mighty shove from below and she was there. "What can you see? Anywhere to get over?" Chris was impatient.

Catherine looked down into what had once been a lovely garden. "It's like a jungle, dreadfully overgrown. There's a house in the distance. I wonder if anyone lives there."

"They certainly do, Miss," a curt voice replied from a tangle of bushes.

"Oh dear, I didn't mean to spy." Catherine was red with embarrassment as the old man backed out of the thicket. He had difficulty in straightening up.

"You are one of the river girls. I've seen you on the boats." His sharp, grey eyes looked accusing under beetling brows. "Don't have many callers out here. Care to see a bit more of the jungle?"

To Catherine, he sounded lonely.

"I'm with a friend." she said doubtfully, looking down at Chris, leaning against the tree, arms folded with eyebrows raised in comic alarm.

"No matter, bring 'em all. See here, follow the wall that way and you'll come to a gate." He peered at his pocket watch, "Any road, it's time for a break." Without waiting for an answer, he stumped off, abandoning his shears on the ground.

Chris caught Catherine when she jumped and they fell together, laughing, in the dry leaves.

"What have you got us into?"

"I think he wants company and I feel awful criticising his garden in front of him. He's old and we needn't stay long."

The gate, really a door, in the wall opened onto a brick path. It ran between rampant rose bushes, some still in flower and tall chrysanthemums, bronze and purple mops bright against the dark foliage. The cottage was covered in creeper and more roses reluctantly allowed space for casement windows under the thatch. The front door was open. Shine on the brass knocker and the polished wood floor were in contrast to the overgrown garden. A smell of wax polish mixed with apples and wood smoke and somewhere in the house, a clock chimed four.

"I would think it was once two cottages," Chris examined the hall with a professional eye.

"Absolutely correct," the voice came from the end of the passage. "Know about architecture?"

"I'm interested, but with the war I joined up like everyone else. Have you lived here long Sir?"

"Family came from these parts. When I retired from the Merchant Service, thought I should return to my roots. Ethel had left me, died you know, so nothing to take me anywhere special."

Captain Morgan sighed and pushed his horn-rimmed spectacles more firmly on his nose.

"It's been a good place to live but I'm stiffer by the day. Too much ground and no one around to help these days, either joined up or in the factories. I'm lucky to have Mrs Mim, good soul that she is, sees me through in the house and I do what I can outside."

He turned back into the kitchen.

"Come along now, kettle's on the boil and there could be a Mrs Mim cake somewhere."

The Captain had put a teapot and mugs on the scrubbed table. A faded setter, grey about the muzzle, lay on a blanket by the dresser.

"Red's even older than me, that's in dog years."

He stirred the dog with his foot.

"On a bad day he won't go far from his bed."

The old dog thumped his tail. Catherine knelt down to stroke him and Red rolled over with pleasure and curled his lip back, grinning.

"He can do with any amount of that."

The Captain was pleased for the dog.

"On a good day we go down through the woods and he'll slosh about in the reed beds. I like to see the goings on up and down the river. Bit rum having women on the boats, but there you go, not the thing in my day."

Over tea, the old man talked of his sea going days. Chris was particularly interested in his tales of the Far East, wondering if his own future might be in those waters. Like Colonel Howard, the old sea Captain followed the progress of the war on a wall map which he used to show Chris the routes he had taken ships as a Master Mariner.

Catherine left the men talking and wandered about the sitting room at the front of the house. The wooden furniture shone, cushions were neatly plumped on armchairs and the sofa, silver and brass gleamed. Everything was well cared for but the room lacked the careless, lived in warmth of the kitchen. She picked up a silver framed photograph of a woman with a kind face, wearing a dropped waist dress belonging to the twenties. There was another of a dark haired, straight-backed man, maybe the Captain, receiving some presentation. The correctness of the room chilled her and she went thankfully into the garden to pick some flowers for the kitchen. She pricked her finger on the spiky roses but picked enough to fill a jug for the kitchen table. The smell was sweet and heady. She poured cold tea, left in the pot, with some milk into Red's bowl.

"Good for your coat, old fellow."

She encouraged him to drink. Washing the mugs and hanging them on the dresser, Catherine wondered how the old dog and his master would manage as their joints became stiffer. Luckily there was a Mrs Mim.

It was dusk when they left the cottage, by the gate leading into the lane.

"Just a mile or two down the road and you'll be in the village."

Captain Morgan carefully packed his pipe with precious tobacco and waved them off.

"Think I'll bring him some duty free tobacco."

Chris linked arms with Catherine.

"That's a super idea, he'd really like that. I wonder how old he is?"

"God knows."

Catherine could not help laughing at such a statement of fact. Then remembering back to the cottage, "When the war is over, will you train as an architect?

Chris did not reply at once and Catherine felt him shiver. "I can't think that far ahead." He quickened their pace. "Come on, we'll be late at the Duck and Feather and I'd hate the others to get a head start on the beer."

Captain Morgan's mile or two stretched on and it was dark when they reached the beginning of the village.

"Not much further," Chris urged and with renewed strength, they ran down the steep hill onto the little hard and into the welcoming arms of the Duck and Feather.

Catherine blinked in the sudden light as they thrust through the blackout curtains into the bar. A thick haze of tobacco smoke hung heavily and the hum of conversation died at their entrance. "Where have you been? Lost in the woods with this wicked wolf? What's the birthday girl going to have?"

They were all there to welcome, Liz and June with Pete and his friend, Mo and Dick and others she knew by sight off the flotillas.

Later in the evening, Pete's friend improvised on the battered piano. His fingers drifted over the keys coaxing accompaniment to favourite songs. Catherine looked round at the noisy group. Pete's arm was round Liz and he looked pleased with himself. Mo and Dick were squeezed into the same armchair. There was so much laughter and ribaldry, a kind of anchor against an uncertain future. She thought of Captain Morgan and Red alone in the cottage. The piano player struck some random chords then rippled into "The sailor with the navy blue eyes".

Someone shouted out, "That's Catherine, happy birthday darling".

To her delight everyone in the bar raised their glasses, "Many happy returns!"

"My hat, what a day," she told Liz later, "I really did feel special".

Then remembering the wood, she added with honesty, "and nearly grown up".

Chapter Six

Throughout the Autumn and into the winter of 1943 the Landing Craft flotillas worked hard. Exercises in home waters, mock landings on the seaward side of the island and on isolated beaches along the south coast, forays across the channel to keep the enemy guessing, meant that all three services worked increasingly as one. Unified by a common aim, the combined services grew in strength and expertise, fulfilling Lord Mountbatten's vision.

The river hummed with activity and the sense of urgency made support staff grudge time away, although shore leave was still available. Anything that happened away from the river lacked reality. Despite this, Mo and June arranged to work a forty-eight hour shift to collect enough time to visit the Farm, June's home. Mo needed help and June hoped she had the answer.

The telephone call came from Gina, a student nurse working in a London suburban Hospital.

"I've been trying to get you all day."

"Well, what's wrong? I can't hear you properly. What are you crying for?"

The relief of hearing her elder sister was too much for Gina.

"Is Mum O.K.?"

Mo was exasperated. She had rushed up to the White House for a quick supper before returning for the evening duty trips. She was hungry and tired.

The line crackled, Gina gulped and regained control.

"Nearly all our end of the street has gone, Mrs Bailey's shop, twenty seven and twenty three as well as ours. Oh Mo, it was a land mine what did it and......." the line crackled again.

Mo gripped the receiver, her knuckles were white and a wave of sickness threatened.

"Mum?" she breathed into the receiver. Then louder, "What about Mum and Tom?"

The interference on the line receded and Gina's voice became stronger.

"Mum and Tom are safe, but they came up from the shelter to nothing, just rubble and space. Mo, all our end has gone. Old Mr Bailey and Grandfather as well."

Gina's voice faltered, "There can't even be a funeral, 'cause there's nothing left".

The warning pips went followed by rattling coins as Gina paid for more time. Don't be cut off, Mo prayed.

"Where are you and where is Mum?"

She longed to hear her mother's voice.

"I'm back at work, the hospital is short handed and Mum made me. Anyway she and Tom are with Aunt Edie and there's no phone, that's why I'm ringing. Mum says not to fuss and she'll be writing."

"Sounds like Mum."

Mo was cross but comforted.

"Look after yourself," she managed to get in before the money ran out.

It was later that evening, driving the Cutter up the dark river, when she realised she would never see her grandfather again.

"He's an old devil, was," she corrected herself to Catherine standing by her side. "But he did do lovely things for me and Gina when we were little. Making a rabbit out of his hankie and playing the galloping major till we laughed so much we fell off his knee. Expect he tried to make up for the awfulness of Dad, especially after he upped and left."

She sighed, "Goods and bads always get so mixed".

Catherine squeezed her arm in sympathy as Mo added, "But he didn't deserve to be blown to bits even if he wouldn't go down the shelter. Why the hell should he have to leave home at his age?"

She broke off remembering there was now no home.

"Blast and damn Hitler," she raged at the dim lines of moored craft and the sea grass bordering the river, pale in the quarter moon.

The familiar throb of the boat engine and gentle protest of water folded back by the Cutter's passage calmed Mo. She rested her head against Catherine's shoulder and let tears come. Catherine realised there was nothing she could say to make Mo better; being there was perhaps enough.

Before bed, June remembering sugar was good for shock, put an extra spoonful in the mug of cocoa. Mo was in her dressing gown, hunched on a stool by the kitchen table.

"Drink up, then try and sleep. I'll cover any emergency trips that crop up."

Mo warmed her hands round the mug, gratefully. "I can't bear to think of them staying in London after all this. They should get the hell out of it; easy to say, but where would they go?"

"I might have the answer," June spoke slowly, thinking aloud. "Briar Cottage must be empty now Len's joined up and I know Jeannie and the baby were going to her parents in Wales."

She thought on, "It's small but furnished and only down the road from the Farm".

She leaned encouragingly towards Mo.

"It could be really good for both our Mums. Yours needs a home and mine could do with another woman's company."

That was the reason behind this sudden visit. Their hitched lift in Yard transport took them to the station and, breathlessly, onto a train just leaving. The monotonous noise and motion lulled them to sleep, exhausted after working a double watch. The carriage filled round them but they slept until the familiar, "Sarsbry 'ere," penetrated June's dreams.

Helped by waiting passengers, eager for seats, they fell out clutching bags and gas masks.

The local train stopped at every little station and in between. Refreshed from sleep, June gave a running commentary on the familiar, to her, landmarks. Mo, gazing at fields of cattle, grazing sheep and ploughed earth, tried to imagine her mother in the midst of so much space.

Patty was waiting for them with the pony and trap.

"The petrol goes nowhere so it has to be Bumble power for short journeys."

June rubbed the nose of the fat pony, standing between the shafts, while Patty stowed their luggage under the bench seat.

"D'you want to drive?" Patty offered the reins to her sister. "Can't wait to leave school and join up." She looked enviously at their uniforms.

"You'll need the parents' permission if you want to go at seventeen and a half," June warned her sixteen-year old sister. "Better start working on Dad; you know he doesn't like any of us leaving the Farm. He likes to plan it as a family concern," she explained to Mo.

"You and James got away, so why shouldn't I?" Patty added, "Did you know James is home, so you two actually overlap this time".

"How super!" June turned to Mo, "I haven't seen him for simply ages and now you'll meet him too".

James had joined the Fleet Air Arm in 1941, a year ahead of June. He was an engineer working on an air station sited in Cornwall. June caught Mo's sleeve and pointed to a flint cottage with a grey slate roof. "Look that's Briar, the garden looks a bit overgrown but that's because nobody's there."

Mo peered over the hedge, spiked with red hips, at the lush grass and gnarled apple trees. Bumble pricked up her ears and broke into a smart trot.

"You greedy thing," Patty told her. "Nearly home and all you want is your feed."

Clattering into the cobbled yard brought people from all directions. June tumbled into her mother's arms; Bridget took charge of Bumble and her twin Rob seized the bags from Patty. Everyone talked at once.

"I'm James and you must be Mo, June's friend from the boats. See, I've heard about you."

The fair, young man with June's brilliant blue eyes, swung Mo easily down from the trap.

"Hope it was good," Mo wondered.

The burly figure of June's father emerged from the big barn.

"Good to have you home, lass. You look well enough. Welcome to your friend Maureen."

He grasped Mo's hand. She felt his strength and hardness but noticed how his eyes softened when he placed a hand on his eldest daughter's shoulder.

"Do you know it's the first time for more than a year that we've all sat round this table together?" June's mother smiled at her family with satisfaction. There were nine to feed that night, including Fay, the land girl. Plenty of home grown vegetables eked out the Hunter's Pot. This was followed by blackberry and apple summer pudding together with a great bowl of junket from the home dairy. Conversations crossed backwards and forwards and round the edge of the table. Mo was drawn into the family talk. She wanted the homely atmosphere for her mother.

Mr and Mrs Miller, both approved June's suggestion. Mr Miller disliked the cottage lying empty and Mrs Miller missed the neighbourliness of Jeannie Stone. Mrs Miller had said tactfully to her husband, "The cottage should not lie empty and Mrs Baker may give me a hand about this place.

Goodness knows there's enough to do".

She was used to negotiating for herself and their children.

One day on the Farm was not enough. Mo looked over Briar Cottage. June and her mother caught up with each other, James was about the Farm with his father, Fay had to see to a sow in farrow. Patty and the twins were away at school, cycling home late, famished and tired.

That evening, Mo sat at the kitchen table, writing to her mother. It was quiet except for the ticking clock and the click of Mrs Miller's knitting needles. Patty was curled in the rocking chair reading, a farm cat clung perilously as she rocked. The twins had gone to bed. James and June were discussing farm business with their father in his study and Fay, having settled the sow with her piglets, was off to the Pig and Whistle to meet a friend.

Mrs Miller looked across at Mo, "May I add a note to your letter? Your mother's had such a rotten time. The quietness of Briar might be just what she and little Tom need". She had been saddened by June's account of the disappearance of Mo's alcoholic father, following Tom's birth. Now the poor woman had lost her own father and her home. She, herself, had worries, two children in the forces, cut backs on the Farm, a husband who was a perfectionist but she felt fortunate compared to Mrs Baker.

The following day June and Mo were on the local train, with James, approaching Salisbury, where it would be all change.

"I hope the letters persuade your Mum and she decides to come."

"I hope so too," Mo replied. "The cottage is lovely but so different from London. Anyway, Tom's safety will count with her I know."

"Take care, Junie, must dash that's my train. See you little Mo." James had gone before there was time to answer.

They had to wait for their connection and the train was overcrowded. They sat on the travel bag in the corridor and were glad of the rock buns provided by June's mother. Inexplicably, the train came to a sudden and lengthy halt outside Southampton.

"We won't have a hope in hell getting back in time." June was gloomy. "And we won't be popular with the other watch."

"Can't be helped. We'll have to make it up to them another time."

Mo's mind was occupied by family problems.

Finally back at Base, all thoughts of families faded. The rush was on to change, get down to the boats and catch up with river life. Drawing breath,

June and Mo waited in the Quartermaster's hut. Catherine and Liz had taken the Cutter to refuel and the Crash boat was away on a compass swinging exercise. The river was empty of Landing Craft.

"Not expected till late afternoon," Stripey told them.

"It's so quiet; I don't know why we hurried," Mo grumbled.

"Never you mind, it's been all go."

He finished rolling the tickler, neatened the tobacco both ends and tucked the finished article into his cap band for a spare.

"One of your Cutters got 'erself stuck on the slipway on a falling tide and young Catherine spent the night waiting for the tide to float 'er. Leastways wasn't 'er fault. Crew of the previous watch made the cat's cradle. And your fella'," he turned to Mo with a wink, "Landed up with wire all round his Craft's prop and had to be towed into the Yard and in the middle of it all Cap'n of Base needed a boat to get urgently up river". He sucked his teeth, "Plenty going on all right".

The second duty cutter came alongside.

"Don't tie up," Stripey shouted down. "A maintenance party's to be collected from t'other side and returned to Yard. After that the flotillas will be back for mooring up."

The Coxswain waved. "Had a good time, you two? Missed you, the river's been wild."

The Cutter, Catherine on the tiller, appeared at the mouth of the river, to be overtaken by the Crash boat. In the distance the first of the returning Landing Craft was visible. The Coxswain, from the other watch, hurriedly handed over the Crash boat, with a "Not before time," admonishment. June waited on deck to watch Catherine bring the Cutter alongside and remarked, "She certainly knows what she's up to".

Mo nodded. "At this rate she'll end up with a boat of her own and I'll have to find another crew." Mo climbed into the Cutter as Liz joined June on the Crash boat.

"Did you hear about the slipway?" Catherine asked anxiously.

"You did the right thing, and it wasn't your fault. Stay where you are, I'll have a go at crewing." Mo pointed at the flotillas. "Looks as if we're in business." Catherine was pink with pleasure.

Chapter Seven

Mist rolled in from the sea. It began like threads of cotton wool and built up as a thick blanket, muffling sound. Liz strained her eyes; ahead was a seemingly solid white wall. Dancing dots, from her own vision, bounced back against the whiteout.

"Keep sounding the fog horn as I creep forward." June's voice, "And tell me the moment you see anything". She throttled down the Crash boat's powerful engines and anxiously peered through the windscreen. She could just make out the dim outline of Liz's legs, astride on the foredeck.

Liz heard the muted swish of water against the bows as June inched forward. There came the mournful clang of a bell.

"Spit buoy dead ahead."

The cumbersome form swam towards them out of the fog. June eased the wheel to starboard and Liz looked down on the massive marker buoy disappearing to port.

"Good, we're spot on. Now keep a look out for the first of the piles."

"God it's thick. I hate fog more than anything. Whoops, there's number one." Liz counted. It was so close she could see barnacles and green weed clinging to the side of the post. A disturbed gull took off from the top with a raucous shriek.

"O.K. for you with wings."

It was a relief to reach the safety of the second trot of moored Landing Craft. The ship's Quarter Master took their lines and June shut off the engines. The wardroom was warm, a contrast to the clammy world outside. Bill, the skipper, had glasses ready in anticipation of their arrival.

"To keep out the cold," he pronounced, pouring liberal tots of gin and, more meanly, added a dash of orange. "You'd better tuck into these, save you trekking up to the Wrenery." He indicated a pile of thickly cut sandwiches.

"You are good to us, Uncle Bill." June smiled as she rubbed her eyes, smarting in the smoky atmosphere. "My eyes feel on stalks with staring. It's so thick out there."

Liz looked round curiously. It was the first time she had visited Bill's boat where June was so obviously at home. There was a photograph pinned to the bulkhead of Bill, without a beard, with his arm round a girl holding a child. It must be his wife and son. It was strange how much younger he looked clean-shaven. She wondered if it was the beard that had earned him the name of uncle. A second photograph was of a stout Labrador crammed behind the wheel of an M.G. sports car.

"That's Meg, one of the girls I left behind." Smithy, Bill's number one, explained from the corner of the cabin where he was sorting signals. "My sister's looking after her for the duration."

"Which? Car or dog?" Liz queried. "Your lab looks as if she ought to be on a diet. Greedy things, Labradors, bad as spaniels." She bit hungrily into a wedge of bread and corned beef. "Our dogs are absolute dustbins, given half a chance."

Smithy laughed at her severe tone. He made room for her on the side bunk. Liz watched him sift through the pile of papers.

"The Mid. Should have done that for you." Bill voiced his disapproval. "You must delegate or he'll never learn." He snapped open his lighter and held the flame to June's cigarette. Their eyes met over the small flame before he changed direction to light up his pipe.

"I take your point but he's doing O.K. Rehearsals for the Christmas Panto are hotting up and he has a part to learn." Smithy excused himself and the Mid. "Doug's been breathing down my neck and we can't have the lad giving the ship a bad name."

Liz gave a guilty start. "Me too," she sighed. "I read my damned lines before I go to sleep. That way it's meant to stick, only I fall asleep and in the morning I can't remember a thing."

"Are you in on the act Juniper?" Bill's pipe crackled and threw out a spark, threatening his beard.

June sipped her drink. "I'm useless at that sort of thing. Your pipe looks as if it could do with a clean." She relaxed enjoying the comfort of Bill's wardroom. She turned to Smithy, "Talking of the Mid, has his toothache gone? Only I wonder if it's a wisdom tooth coming".

Smithy laughed. "Not likely to be anything connected with wisdom. But ask him yourself," he added, as a boy in Midshipman's uniform appeared in the door way.

"I'm starving; learning makes me hungry."

"Just a growing lad." Smithy teased.

"Better get yourself off to check tomorrow's orders with the Bosun," Bill interrupted, shortly.

"It must be hard to be the bottom of the pecking order," Liz remarked to June as the Crash boat drew away from the side of the Landing Craft.

"Well that's a Mid's lot, but Bill is very fair." June was loyal. "He has got high standards and there's not much that escapes him. But he's very popular with his crew. Sparks says the lads will do anything for him and there's proof as no one ever asks for a transfer." She broke off pointing to the outline of the jetty. "Thank goodness the fog's lifting," she added more quietly to herself. "Uncle Bill's a great guy when you get to know him."

"I wonder a bit about June and Bill." Liz soaking in a hot bath, voiced her concern to Catherine, who wrapped in a towel, was waiting to leap in after her. The hot tank at Pantiles did not fill many baths.

"Well, he makes no secret that he's married and has a little boy. June's friendly with the whole ship. She must know what she's doing. Hurry up or the water will run cold."

"It's the way they look and share special jokes. He's a bit smooth and it would be awful if she got hurt." Liz got out to dry herself.

"Ooh heavenly." Catherine luxuriated in the bath. "Expect he's lonely, missing his wife, and June likes looking after people. Should we hear each others parts before we get our heads down?"

Liz groaned. "I wish I hadn't such a big part. Much more fun to be a tartlet in the chorus."

The Knave of Hearts, produced by the Base, for the Base, was a pantomime come revue. The material was drawn from day to day incidents well known to Cormorant and the flotillas. Pete and Doug were the producers, responsible for the script, casting and stage management. Pete gave Liz a star part, because of her looks and in the hope that he would see more of her. She worked hard at her lines and was a glamorous princess but remained indisputably Liz. Catherine had more fun in the chorus but Mo became the real star of the show.

"She's a natural and so funny. Great casting as the knave. Yes sir, that little red head is a load of dynamite." Doug and Pete checked over the script, one evening, in the Duck and Feather.

"What d'you think of Liz? Doesn't she just look the part of the Princess?"

"Looks O.K. but as soon as she opens her mouth you know she's Roedean. Can't act for toffee. Still we're not going to get it all right with a bunch of amateurs." Doug sighed for his pre war repertory days.

"Cheltenham Ladies, in fact," Pete put him right. "Fill em up, Josie dear, just time for one more before closing."

The door of the Duck and Feather shut, cutting them off from the warmth and intimacy of the bar. The night was clear and frosty with a full moon and myriad stars. The river, at half ebb, exposed narrow margins of mud, glistening in the cold light.

"A bomber's moon." As Pete spoke, so came the distant wail of a siren.

"Bloody hell, looks as if we're in for a party. Must get back on board to receive the buggers."

Doug ran down the alley, leading to the catamarans and landing stage. The floating catamarans jerked unevenly under their hurrying feet. The Cutter waited, engine idling, in darkness alongside. Navigation lights were forbidden during air raids.

"You nearly missed us. I was about to cast off," Catherine's cheerful voice came from the bows.

Pete and Doug joined the small group of passengers waiting to be returned to their ships. Catherine stayed forward to keep a look out. Journeying without lights could be hazardous.

Most passengers were bound for Craft moored up river, so were delivered first. They heard the uneven throb of enemy aircraft as they made their way down river. Ragged clouds now obscured the moon and search lights' probing fingers made intricate patterns across the dark sky. Ack-ack fire broke out in sharp staccato from the lines of Landing Craft. Sparks streaming upwards reminded Catherine of childhood firework parties.

"Can't you go any faster?" Doug was desperate to be on board and join in.

"Nearly there and Catherine put on your tin hat in case of falling shrapnel."

Mo took the Cutter alongside and Doug thankfully clambered aboard. "It's your last trip, so hang about and join in" he suggested.

Catherine had a different view of the river from the gun turret. The stream of live bullets, deceptively brilliant, was the flotillas angry response to the invaders of their air space. But it was the extreme concentration and synchronisation of Doug's gunnery crew that held her attention.

"Not our lucky night." Doug was disappointed as the bombers slipped away. "Hope they won't do too much damage."

"At least Mum and Tom aren't in London anymore." Mo thought comfortably of them tucked up in Briar Cottage.

Doug's surge of adrenaline died down as he remarked, seeing Mo and Catherine's faces, tired and pale under the severe tin hats.

"Cuppa's all round before you go to your moorings."

The girls looked so young and vulnerable, not much more than kids.

The all clear sounded while they waited on the mooring for the Pierhead duty boat. All was quiet; the river slept.

There was so much going on. Pantomime rehearsals, hockey matches, impromptu parties on the ships, and work, the reason they were there at all. The winter brought rough seas and biting winds, work intensified with more duties within the river and longer trips away. Cormorant increased the Wren complement again. The Boat Officer issued duffle-coats against the cold, commissioned more small boats and promoted some seasoned deckhands to coxswains. Catherine collected a hook and, as a leading wren coxswain, gained a boat. Liz was transferred to be her stoker and crew.

"They always leave when they've become really useful," Mo moaned.

"Well, I'm sad Liz is moving. But I'm pleased for Catherine to have someone so superbly efficient and dependable. It's quite tough starting off in a boat of your own."

The boat, a carvel built cutter with a kelvin engine and kitchener gear was lying on a slipway across the river.

"The Maintenance crew are getting her ready. But you could have her sooner if you go across and put some of the paint on yourselves."

The Boat Officer's advice was perhaps prophetic.

"Useful that she's out of the water. We can see the whole of her, above and below the water line."

Catherine took her new responsibility seriously.

"I'm trying to remember how a kitchener gear works." Liz was thinking of the engine.

"There are so many angles to a boat and whatever position I'm in I can't get it right. And the paint is so drippy."

The paint shop had issued brushes and white paint for the inside of the boat. Fortunately, the anti fouling had been done.

"Maybe we'll improve with practice."

Liz was slightly neater than Catherine. But it was with relief that they finished the job and returned the brushes and empty tins to the paint store.

The Store-man looked them over.

"Was it the boat you were painting?" he could not help asking.

"It is the first time," Catherine defended their efforts.

"Have you got more turps?" Liz asked. "We'll need baths in the stuff."

The newly painted boat left the slipway, immaculate. Overall, she was similar to the other cutters, strong reliable boats with Ford engines. The difference was the Kelvin engine and kitchener gear. The engine started easily but from the beginning the design of gear wheel, incorporating the throttle, was a problem.

Liz quickly developed a love hate relationship, which was in danger of turning to pure hate.

"I've never, simply never ever come across such a contrary contraption in my life."

She eyed the wheel warily.

"When it's in a mood it takes the strength of Samson to shift, other times it hardly takes a touch. No warning either way. I am trying not to get a thing about it," she told Catherine, "And I won't be beaten. It's got to do what I want".

Her jaw set firmly.

The further side of the river was the scene of the final battle. A crisp winter morning when the sun was beginning to burn off the overnight frost, Catherine sniffed the air like a hound tuned in to the country. She felt good to be where she was at that instant in time. She turned to share her happiness with Liz but her taut figure and tense face told her no.

Liz was concentrating on the problem that now dominated her life. How would the gear behave today? Wren stoker colleagues were not helpful. They were not experienced in Kelvins and kitcheners and the male stoker, at the Pier-head could only advise brute force or returning it as junk. Either course would admit defeat.

Catherine took the Cutter between the moored boats and positioned to run into the jetty. Quite a crowd of expectant passengers waited their arrival.

"Ease down," she gave Liz the usual order.

Nothing happened. The engine retained its full throaty roar.

Liz, purple, gripped the gear wheel. Using all her strength, she turned the wheel to throttle down before taking it that bit further which should disengage the gear into neutral. Nothing happened. The wheel refused to move.

"Come on," Liz implored through gritted teeth.

Catherine, abandoning any idea of stopping, swept past the amazed bystanders and in a wide circle, at full speed, returned to the main stream. She had a fleeting impression of a sea of faces, mouths agape, following their passage as the cutter sped past.

The second run in was also doomed to failure, despite hefty blows with a spanner from Liz's tool kit. This time, a cheer went up from the jetty and some joker shouted, "Great performance Stokes. What price a trip across the river?" Liz was mortified.

Catherine could not let it happen again.

"You must stall the engine and if only I can judge it right, we'll get alongside. Third time lucky." Liz understood.

"Cut!"

As the engine died, Liz scrambled to the bows and waited, ready with boathook and line. It was very quiet with no engine, only the swish of water sounded against the hull as the boat continued, inexorably, towards the jetty where the now silent group watched and waited.

Catherine spoke to the boat. "Slowly, more slowly, we mustn't overshoot."

They were level. Liz flung the line, caught by someone and a swift turn round a bollard. Catherine threw the stern line into a friendly hand, another swift turn and the boat was arrested.

"Nice bit of boat handling, hooky," Catherine was congratulated.

"Kitchener gears are notoriously difficult. She'd better go back for a complete overhaul. I'll have a word with your Bosun."

Liz recognised the Commander of the Base coming on board, followed by a Yard engineer.

"Proper devils they can be, Sir."

The engineer turned to Liz. "Let's see if I can shift the monster." Liz felt slightly mollified.

The Cutter was returned to the Maintenance team. Never reliable, she remained a reserve for river work. Catherine remarked sadly, "She was O.K. going along just no good at arriving."

She and Liz both loved her replacement, a thirty five footer with a petrol engine amidships. The steering wheel was positioned forward with no remote engine control. This meant Liz stayed controlling the engine in response to Catherine's signals. This was most satisfying and required good team work.

Chapter Eight

"It will be my first Christmas away from home." Catherine sucked her piece of orange dry at half time. "There will be no stockings or church in the morning, no walking off Christmas dinner or silly games in the evening."

Chris leaned on his hockey stick. "I haven't been home for Christmas in ages, so I suppose I've got used to not being there, expect my parents have too. Will you mind?"

"I'd hate not being here. Besides the first performance of the Knave is on Boxing Day; I must be here for that. But I wonder what will happen at Christmas. Will it be different from any other day?"

"Expect the ships will drink their way through Christmas and into New Year, some to celebrate and others to drown their sorrows," Chris predicted. "Come on, it's the second half, dusk already even though we're in half summer time."

The idea slowly grew in Catherine's mind. "If I can't be home for Christmas, I might squeeze in a swift visit before." She wanted to include Liz. "I'd love you to come too. We could work two watches and take forty eight hours."

At the last moment Liz changed her mind.

"Honestly, I'd love to have come, but Gran's been ill and I just think I should be there to cheer them up."

Going to look, Liz knew, was her best reassurance that all was well.

"No she can't come after all." Catherine rang home. "Well I didn't know till now. Her Grandmother's ill. No, I don't know what's wrong. She'd love to come another time. Yes, of course I'm coming. I'm looking forward to it."

As usual the telephone conversation with her mother was vaguely unsatisfactory and left her feeling in the wrong. She replaced the receiver and shrugged.

"Well it will be lovely to see Dad and the boys."

Catherine boarded a bus at the station. The familiar streets bore unfamiliar scars. Jagged walls and disrepair were sad reminders of a yesterday's home. Catherine was startled by the bomb damage.

"Home on leave, ducks?" The woman conductor noted Catherine's interest and uniform.

"That was part of a stick of bombs Gerry got rid of in a hurry. Chased by one of our spitfires, he machine gunned all the way down Western Road before making off out to sea where he bloody well copped it himself. And serve him right. Fares please."

She stumped off down the gangway, aggressively clicking her ticket puncher. "Lord sakes, wait till the bus stops." She restrained an elderly man. "He'll end up with a broken leg and no mistake."

She kept up a running commentary for her captive audience, a mixture of mother hen and sergeant major. Catherine pinged the bell for the next stop.

Her heart lifted at the sight of her own home, still intact, on the corner opposite the Park entrance. The front gate was missing, her father's contribution towards arming the country, and the narrow flowerbeds supported winter cabbages, otherwise no changes. The curtains next door twitched slightly. Catherine smiled; Aunty Madgwick was on the lookout. Alec opened the door before she had time to ring; he pulled her across the threshold and shouted.

"Sam, she's come."

His voice, beginning to break, was husky and ended in a squeak.

"Kettle's on."

Sam's deeper voice came from the kitchen.

"Mum's at the factory, but should be home any minute. You haven't much luggage."

Alec pushed his horn-rimmed spectacles more firmly on his blob of a nose.

"Does the white lanyard mean you work on boats? And did you sew that blue anchor on your arm when you were promoted?"

"Alec, give me a chance."

The house smelt the same, of polish and aromatic geranium plants wintering indoors on north facing sills. Catherine hung her gas mask and great-coat on a hook by the front door, next to the boys' raincoats, odd scarves and her father's flat cap for weekends. She went down the passage, past the sitting room, with faded chintz covered chairs and the polished ebony piano supporting framed family photographs, no changes there. The kitchen was warm and inviting. Sam had pushed the table against the dresser, to make room round the boiler. Catherine, found herself in the wicker chair, while Alec perched on the table, swinging his legs.

Sam took up position astride the upright wheel-back. He crossed his arms along the back and leaned towards Catherine, raising his eyebrows quizzically.

"Now, sweet Cat, just fill us in. What exactly have you been up to? Any letters have been useful weather reports, graphic descriptions of sea state, wind and tide. But what about the people? How goes jolly jack tar? Don't tell me there aren't a few lads queuing for our Cat's attention."

Catherine recognised the same old teasing Sam, half serious but digging and delving until it was easier to tell.

"It's difficult to explain because I've never been anywhere or done anything like this before."

She began slowly but was encouraged by their interest. The dusk of the day crept into the room and the open front of the boiler glowed strongly in contrast. Catherine talked on, describing her spent night on the shingle bank, the kitchener gear episode, stormy trips, climbing into Pantiles without a late pass, mooring up the Landing Craft and more of the life on the river. She surprised herself and they were good listeners.

"What did you do on your birthday?" Alec questioned.

"I spent a super evening with friends in the Duck and Feather. Liz, Mo, June and lots of others were there. They even drank my health."

Catherine chuckled at her recollection of the sailor with the navy blue eyes. She kept the walk in the woods with Chris to herself.

The front door closed. Alec jumped off the table.

"That's Mum."

Quick footsteps came down the passage. Sam drew the heavy curtains before switching on the light.

"Darling, I'm so sorry to be late. We ran over time at the factory and then it was ages before I caught a number seven home. But the boys were here."

Catherine, blinking in the sudden light, moved towards her mother and lifted her face for the expected kiss. Mrs Tenant rested a cool cheek against her daughter's, holding her close for a moment. She removed her headscarf and took possession of the basket chair.

"Lordy I'm tired. Alec, be an angel and give me a cup of tea. Sam, you might turn the oven on, there's a casserole to heat for supper. Catherine, why don't you change out of your uniform and put on something that's more like you."

She kicked off her shoes and stretched her toes to the warmth of the boiler. Catherine, disappointed, looked back as she left the room. Her mother's response had been so different to Sam's and Alec's enthusiasm. But then her mother, lying back in the chair, was probably tired after a long day at work.

Catherine shared a bedroom with her sister, at the back of the house. She looked down on the shadowy garden with the patch of grass, narrow beds and broad vegetable plot at the end. Her father had been busy. She drew the curtains, carefully overlapping to avoid chinks of light and turned on the lamp between the twin beds. Helen smiled at Catherine from her photograph, attractive and business like in Nurses uniform against a backcloth of white flat roofed buildings.

"Miss you," Catherine told her. "Wonder what it's like in so much sand and heat."

Helen was somewhere in the Middle East, behind the advancing Allied Army.

Presently Catherine heard her father's key in the front door and taking the stairs, two at a time, she was there to welcome him as he entered.

"Whoa, steady there. Let's see if you've changed."

He stood back, his eyes smiling his delight. He looked his second daughter over and saw the childlike contours of her face had taken a sharper, more adult mould. The questioning look was still there, though, as if she could not quite come to terms with life's absurdities.

Catherine sniffed the tobacco from her father's pipe and the musty train smell, clinging to his city clothes, after the long journey from his office. She was startled by his angular body, with not an ounce of spare flesh, and saddened by the new lines etched on his face.

They ate in the kitchen, the best used room since fuel rationing. The rabbit casserole was tasty. Mrs Tenant enjoyed cooking and the stricture of rationing gave her a challenge. Recovering some of her energy, she entertained them with anecdotes from the factory floor, reminding Catherine what good company her mother was, when she so minded. At the end of the meal, Catherine lit a spill through the bars of the boiler and held it to her father's pipe. She could hear her mother strumming on the piano and knew her father would follow to relax and enjoy a smoke.

Alec helped clear, then pushed off to bed while Sam and Catherine washed up. La Boheme replaced the Moonlight Sonata which in turn was taken over by Madame Butterfly. But the pianist began to make mistakes. The piano lid slammed followed by hurried footsteps mounting the stairs, then running water.

"She's having a bath, that'll help her relax," Sam commented wisely. "Come on Cat, let's have a drink at the Anchor. I fancy a beer and you can tell me more of the river's mud-larks."

"What about Dad?"

Catherine did not want to leave him on his own. But he was asleep and looked peaceful. She kissed him, lightly, on the top of his head and rescued the warm pipe from where it had fallen on his chest.

Sam took her arm in the dark street and she automatically adapted to his uneven gait. He had been part of the family as long as she could remember, like a brother, yet her parents were Uncle Bob and Aunt Kitty to him. Catherine knew that her mother, devastated by her twin sister's death, was particularly fond of Sam. Of them all, he was the one who could break into her mother's sometimes desolate moods, times when she, as a child, crept away to the end of the garden and waited for the sun to shine again.

The Anchor was empty except for a group of older men round the bar.

"The Canadians will fill the place up later," Sam predicted. "Find a table and I'll get the drinks." He went to the bar and spoke to several of the men.

"Art college broken up yet?" Catherine heard the bar man ask. She wondered if Sam came in often. He could be lonely with many of his friends gone.

Sam placed the frothing tankards on the table. "A new barrel, so it's lively. Jim says it'll take a while to settle."

Catherine dug out a packet of blue liners from her sling bag.

"Have one of these while we wait."

Sam lit a match, shielding the flame; Catherine remembered his habit of losing lighters. His hands were slender, those of an artist and his long bony fingers were stained in places by paint.

"Tell me about the College, Sam. Is it good for you? Is there much to learn?"

"It's O.K."

He drew reflectively on his cigarette.

"There is a hell of a lot to learn. But how bloody long will it be before our designs are any use. Building up instead of knocking down, eh?"

He leaned his head on his arms and looked up, dark intelligent eyes under raised eyebrows which merged into his shock of black hair.

"This wastage of bricks and bodies, how and when will it end?"

Catherine thought of the river with the flotillas and busy maintenance yard. Men and women working hard to launch the new offensive, when would they be ready? Her picture of the war was different to Sam's. She caught at Sam's sleeve.

"Do you wish you could be more in things, like Helen and me?"

His reply was lost as the Canadians exploded into the Anchor.

"End of serious talk. Best drink up if you want the other half. This hard drinking mob will clean out the pub in no time."

Sam acknowledged the noisy crowd.

Later, back in the kitchen, sharing a bedtime pot of tea, her father answered for Sam in his absence.

"Life's not easy for anyone different."

Her father dunked his ginger snap and savoured the softened biscuit.

"Sam's bound to feel out of it right now with you and Helen away, but he's a thinking chap and will manage long term. Suffering can make people more understanding, if they don't become bitter and end up with a chip."

He caught Catherine stifling a yawn. "Mustn't keep you up, you'll be needing your sleep after all that work on the boats. Really proud of my two daughters, I am."

"Oh Dad, I'm a fraud when I think of everything you do, travelling to London every day, fire watching in the City at weekends, and Home Guard duties here." Catherine thought but did not add, "And keeping Mum level".

She left him to riddle the boiler, empty the ashes and lock up.

Catherine drew back her curtains. The clouds had cleared, shadows under the trees and shrubs filled the garden with mystery in the moonlight. White rime from hoar frost was already visible on the grass. Aunty Madgwick's tabby crouched on the roof of her shed, fluffed up against the cold, waiting for his enemy the ginger tom from two gardens away. Her bed was warm and inviting. Someone had filled a hot water bottle. It could have been her mother. Did suffering help understanding? She was too sleepy to work it out.

The noise of grumbling cats merged with her dreams. She was on the river in the Cutter filled with Canadians. Sam stood in the bows waving a boathook like a magician's wand. Liz was blowing a fog-horn which became the wailing notes of the air raid siren. Catherine was awake and in her bedroom.

"Bring a blanket and come down. Gerry's been too attentive lately."

Her father was at her door. Alec and her mother were already huddled under the stairs. Sam appeared holding two packs of cards.

"Care for a game of Rummy? Although strip poker might be more in order, seeing our attire. Anyway let's play the night away."

Mrs Tenant pulled her blanket tightly around and shut her eyes.

"I hope your father won't be long next door. Mrs Madgwick is so deaf she won't be worried."

Sam dealt the cards for the three players.

"I think you're collecting the same thing as me," Alec accused Sam crossly. At that moment they heard the uneven note of enemy aircraft. It came like an irregular heart beat, pulsing overhead. Catherine saw her mother open her eyes and her father, back from next door, stand up uncertainly. No one spoke as they heard the sharp patter of anti-aircraft fire followed by a muffled explosion some way off. Catherine caught her breath and braced herself against the wall. Sam shuffled the cards and dealt again.

There were no more explosions and gun-fire became sporadic then died away.

"Let's hope that's all and we can get back to our beds, where Alec certainly ought to be instead of playing cards until all hours."

Catherine caught the disapproval in her mother's voice.

Sam winked at her. "Proper little gambler he'll turn out, even if the currency is only match sticks."

"Yes well."

Her mother was disarmed by Sam's amusement. She kissed Catherine goodnight as if it was the beginning instead of two thirds through.

Catherine's bed was cold, she did not feel sleepy and the enormity of war and destruction pressed in on her

"Oh God," she prayed to the comforting God of her childhood, "Help us through."

Unbidden, came the thought, the enemy probably offered a similar petition.

"What a fix to be God," she announced to no one in particular.

She woke to a change in the weather. The wind had risen and storm clouds resembling grey galleons sailed across the sky.

"Let's look at the sea."

Alec was on holiday and had energy to spare. They walked through the Park where tall trees bent to the tune of the wind. There were few people out. The street leading to the sea front gave a little protection and then they were at the mercy of the gale. Catherine looked over the tangle of barbed wire at the turbulent sea.

"Bet you're glad you aren't on it."

Alec had to shout to be heard above the noise of the wind and crashing waves.

"How about you?" Catherine yelled back.

"Not for me. I'm going into the R.A.F. the moment I can."

Catherine looked into his serious face and at the blob of a nose, reddened by the wind.

"Please let it be over before then," was her silent answer.

Sam and Alec saw her off on the train. Her bag was heavier by several packages.

"Not to be opened before Christmas," her mother ruled.

Sam had the last word, as the train gathered momentum.

"Come again soon Cat and in the meantime don't break too many hearts."

She could not say but knew that part of her heart would always be with them.

"How was it?" Liz asked.

"Like the Curate's egg, good in parts," seemed the apt answer for Catherine. "And you?"

"Gran's fine. But good in parts was a bit the same for me. The place was simply swarming with Yanks. They'd taken over everything including Grandpa. Not that he was complaining. He was full of it all. I suppose it reminded him of the Regiment." Liz sighed pleasurably. "Isn't it great to be back. Hope we haven't missed too much. Christmas is only a week away."

Chapter Nine

"If we took our bikes across the river in the duty boat, we'd be saved miles of cycling. We'd have time to give Captain Morgan his presents, wish him a happy Christmas and be back for supper."

Liz agreed with Catherine's plan. It was Christmas Eve and they were on duty at noon Christmas Day so there was little time to spare. Unfortunately it was half tide. However, the Quarter Master helped them carry their bicycles down the slippery steps at Pier-head, into the cutter.

"What are you taking?" The Wren Coxswain pointed to Catherine's bulging saddle bag, now streaked with green slime from the steps.

"Some nutty Liz had from the Yanks at her grandparents, gardening gloves I managed on a clothing chit, a tin of duty free tobacco from Chris, and, best of all," there was pride in Catherine's voice, "A beef bone for Red, from the galley. Not a bad haul."

Captain Morgan was at the front of his cottage reasoning with a rebellious rose. He straightened up.

"Bless me if it isn't Catherine."

He put down the secateurs.

"Who's come with you this time?"

"This is Liz; she's a stoker and my friend. Chris is on leave so he couldn't be here. We've come to wish you and Red a happy Christmas." Catherine's heart lurched. "Where is Red? Is he's all right?"

"He's been with me most of the afternoon watch and has only just sloped off to his basket, wily old blighter, knows when he's had enough." The Captain wiped his hand on the seat of his trousers and shook Liz's. "So this is a friendly stoker." He twinkled at her.

"What a lovely place to live. Any chance of some tea? The ride's made me horribly thirsty."

Liz offered one of her engaging smiles.

Catherine hurried ahead into the cottage, anxious to find Red. All was clean and orderly, evidence of Mrs Mim's attention. Red was asleep in his basket by the stove in the kitchen. The old dog could not hear well but lifted his head when he sensed her presence. Catherine fondled him, feeling his prominent old bones through the silky hair.

"You are a lovely lad," she told him and he lifted a front paw to ask for more.

"Mrs Mim has baked a special cake for Christmas with extra fruit sent by her nephew in America. Think it'll go down well this tea time?"

Captain Morgan eased himself into the chair with arms and beamed at the two girls.

"Didn't know we'd be having a party, eh boy?"

He stirred the dog with his foot. Red thumped his tail in response.

After tea, while the Captain showed Liz photographs of the ships sailed under his command, Catherine made herself busy. She collected the presents from her saddle bag and put them by Mrs Morgan's photograph in the sitting room. Red's prize bone went on the stone shelf in the larder.

"You mustn't open your presents till the morning and don't forget Red's bone."

Captain Morgan nodded vaguely over the pile of photographs.

Dusk had arrived when they started back.

"You'll need your lamps tonight." The Captain checked them over. "Looks like a cloudy night, at least it'll keep the Hun away." He opened the gate. "Give my best to that young fellow of yours, and thank him for the baccy."

"Happy Christmas," they shouted, pedalling away.

Their lamps confined by regulation shields, threw tiny arcs of light on the ground directly below but were useless lighting the way ahead. A segment of moon emerged from thinning clouds as they reached the village and usefully lit the cobbles down to the hard. They had to put on speed to catch the waiting duty boat. Pulling their bicycles across the floating catamarans they just made it.

A full tide flowed strongly to the edges of the sea grass meadows and the air was sharp and cold with a salty tang from the sea. Catherine gazed up at a particularly bright star in the west.

"It should be in the East," she objected. Then, suddenly caught by the magic of Christmas Eve, she said, "I'm really glad we come on duty tomorrow and will be officially on the river for Christmas".

"And I'm glad you took me to see your old Captain, he's a duck," Liz replied as they lifted their bikes easily onto the jetty, level with the cutter at high tide. "Come on, I'm starving, we'll be late for supper if we don't put our skates on."

Mo was already in the Dining room.

"I've been on the phone to Mum. No Christmas leave for Gina but Tom and Mum will be up at the Farm tomorrow. I think she misses the bustle of London but she gets on really well with June's mum." She sighed wanting to be there too. "Bloody hell, not much more than a sniff of meat in this, they'll turn us into vegetables."

"What do you expect with the real blow out tomorrow?" the exhausted steward snapped back from the serving hatch.

"O.K., O.K., no hard feelings, it smells good enough for another spoonful."

Mo did not wish to upset the galley.

"You boats-crew are always hungry."

The mollified steward scraped round the dish and shut the hatch on them.

Christmas Day dawned grey and overcast. Catherine lay in the bottom bunk and allowed her sleepy mind to wander. Waking at home with Helen, whispering in the dark, shifting feet to make stockings at the end of the bed rustle, luminous clock hands creeping so slowly until it was time to open presents. The springs of the bunk above protested as Liz landed on the floor.

"Happy Christmas, old fruit."

They swapped packages, blue enamel ear-rings for Catherine and a book of Favourite Spaniels for Liz. Catherine was surprised and delighted by her presents from home, warm gloves from her parents and a Dorothy Sayers, pocket knife from Alex and a picture by Sam from her bedroom window complete with Aunty Madgwick's moggy on the roof of the shed.

"Your Sam is jolly talented."

Liz held the painting at arm's length. She was delighted with the framed photograph of her father as a young man from her grandparents. She let Catherine try on the pearls sent by her mother.

Present swapping made them late for breakfast, so only time for toast and margarine.

"Maybe as well in view of the feast to come," Catherine remarked.

"We've taken a lot ashore, but the river is quiet now," the retiring watch reported. "So you should get your Christmas lunch O.K."

Stripey, duty Q.M., dozing by the stove in his hut following a liquid lunch, had no special trips lined up.

"Don't matter what you do as long as the duty trips are on time."

The tradition in the Navy is for the officers to serve Christmas dinner to the men under their command. Wrens on any mess deck would only enhance the occasion, so the river wrens did not lack invitations. The problem was which to accept. Catherine and Liz had decided on Uncle Bill's. As Liz observed, "Uncle Bill will go flat out to make it fun and as he is so popular with his crew most of them will be there."

Chris was on leave, to the pleasure of his unspoilt parents, so Catherine had no conflict of interest. Pete, lovelorn for Liz, was on duty at the Base, so well occupied. June when she heard, was delighted, saying, "The more the merrier".

On the way to Bill's Craft, Mo and Stephie, her crew, were dropped at Doug's. Mo proudly showed off a long scarf wound round and round.

"My present from Mum. It must have taken hours and hours of knitting. She said it gave her something to do in the shelter during the blitz."

"What a labour of love."

Catherine was impressed. She could not imagine her own mother dedicating so much time to her, under the stairs at home.

Liz hung on to the side of Doug's Landing Craft and bestowed one of her idyllic smiles.

"Bet you're pleased Dick's on leave."

"Cheeky monkey." Doug winked at Liz as he swung Mo on board and helped Stephie scramble up the side. "What a monstrous muffler." He told Mo. "It'll keep us both warm."

"You are hot stuff already so you don't need any extra heat."

Mo turned to Stephie solemnly.

"You've got to watch him all the way. He'll gobble up innocent little wrens for breakfast given half a chance."

"Absolutely, and small red heads are the most appetizing," Doug's amused comment came swiftly.

"Those two are crazy, they spark each other off. Dick doesn't do that to Mo," Liz said as she joined Catherine.

"Well, Dick's more serious. But then he's older and maybe Mo looks up to him."

Catherine thought, "She might not act the fool with Dick because she wants to impress him more as a woman and not a comic turn."

"But does Dick really see her as she is?" Liz wasn't sure. "I think in a real relationship you have to be liked for what you are."

"If I'm not sure of me, how could any one else; it's all a bit of a muddle."

Catherine felt confused.

Bill's ship was in sight and Liz took her place by the engine, ready to come alongside. She wondered idly if Pete had any idea of the real her. She thought, "Men want to look rather than listen." She tossed her head and pushed a strand of hair out of her eyes. "It would have to change with anyone for keeps, to be truly myself and keep their love. Like it is with Gran and Grandpa. Like it was with Dad."

She stopped thinking and jammed the gear lever into neutral, suddenly aware of Catherine's insistent command on the bell.

Martin, the Midshipman, was waiting. There was a sprig of mistletoe tucked behind his left ear and an imprint of lipstick on his cheek.

"You haven't wasted any time," Catherine accused as he accepted the bow-line.

Liz handed up the line astern and switched off the engine.

"Just getting into the swing."

Martin led the way below, towards an appetising smell of food.

June's flushed face appeared at the entrance to the galley, hot from helping.

"Great, you've come at just the right time. Bill and Smithy and everyone are waiting and we're about to dish up, aren't we?"

The Cook's scarlet face framed in steam was behind her flanked by a hovering seaman waiting to transport dishes.

"Now for it," Liz whispered, her eyes dancing with amusement.

Coloured signal bunting draped over bulkheads and a long table covered with sheets, creases defined by iron-mould, tried to disguise the Mess deck. Most of the crew were there, standing about awkwardly.

"Help," murmured Catherine. "It looks more like a Wake than a Christmas party."

Bill, crowned with a Chef's hat, was sharpening a carving knife and chatting up Stokes and a very young, not very able, seaman, recently joined the ship's company. Bill was doing most of the talking. Smithy pounced with relief.

"Have a gin and orange; drink's the best ice breaker."

He drained his own tumbler and splashed in a refill.

Bill's banter, Smithy's attention to their glasses and the presence of the Wrens changed the atmosphere. Catherine and Liz, mindful they were on duty, refused Smithy's third block buster. As the party got underway, the jokes became increasingly bawdy and the applause was universal and deafening when Martin made his entrance dressed as a fairy, supposedly from the top of the tree. He pirouetted round the flaming pudding brought in by Smithy. Suddenly, Jock the dour gunner liberally laced with alcohol and egged on by his mates, picked Martin up like a child and set him on the top of the table. Martin executed a couple of toe taps round the dishes, knocked a glass flying and with an enormous, froglike leap regained the deck. Pursued by a stream of earthy jokes, he fled to the safety of the wardroom.

A lengthy bout of health drinking followed.

"Too many absent friends," was Liz's verdict.

Stokes then produced his mouth organ and lulled the party into sentimental mood.

"Sorry, really must go or we'll be late."

Catherine clutched at Liz as they escaped from too many loving embraces to the sanctuary of their boat.

"A pity you have to leave."

Bill saw them away.

"June's joining us in the wardroom for a sobering down session."

"It's lucky for June, having the Crash boat on the slips for maintenance."

Liz took gulps of cool air as an antidote to the fug she had left.

"Well, I'd had enough and we had a good excuse to come away."

Catherine surveyed the peaceful river.

"Shouldn't think we'll have many passengers as most shore goers are already there and I bet those left on board will be getting their heads down."

It was quiet and in between duty trips Catherine and Liz repaired to the Q.M.'s hut. Thick dark tea which stewed forever on the top of his stove was good for a hangover. Catherine drained her mug.

"It's all so quiet, I don't think there'll be any more excitement, do you?"

She sounded disappointed. Stripey rolled his tickler with practised skill.

"Well, see here, it's like the law of averages." He paused to lick and seal the cigarette paper. "A lot 'o the lads went ashore during morning watch and they'll be back this side of midnight."

Liz held her lighter for him; he puffed reflectively and looked across at Catherine, warming her hands round the stove pipe.

"And, I ask myself, what have they been doing with themselves. There's a lot of hours between then and what's to come. That's all I say."

Mo opened the door to hear the last of his words.

"Nothing can be as bad as facing a mess deck of amorous sailors, frustrated and far from home. Where's the tea? Stephie and I are parched from too much alcohol and fending off lover boys."

As it grew dark the river woke to life. The two duty boats were kept busy taking passengers from ship to ship and more from shore to ship. They were showered with invitations from more than happy men.

Liz groaned, "It's one long ship crawl for everyone but us."

"Thank goodness it's nearly midnight." Catherine yawned hugely. "That should be our last trip tonight."

They followed Mo and Stephie's open cutter up river and took position outside them, alongside the floating jetty, crowded with waiting sailors. There were the usual catcalls and ribaldry but on the whole the mood was quiet.

Men clambered across the open cutter into Catherine's boat.

"Sit down and keep the boat balanced." Catherine was firm. "That's it, no more this time round." About to cast off, she heard a commotion far down the line of floating cats leading to the alley. "Don't let go Liz, we'd better see what's to do."

A gigantic, alcoholic sailor, red from Christmas cheer, reeled unsteadily towards the boats. Brandishing a bottle in each hand he told the world, "I belang in Glasgie, dear auld Glasgie tu......"

The waiting passengers instinctively drew back, clearing a path. The massive Scotsman, continuing in song, lurched through the throng and swayed at the edge of the catamaran. The entire company held their breath, hypnotised by the drunken giant who waved his bottles, taking a final swig before gathering himself to leap, blindly, aboard the open cutter. The engine casing splintered at the impact of the heavy body and there he lay, out for the count, in the middle of Mo's Ford V 8. No one could shift him.

"He'll have to sleep it off where he is."

Mo's decision was reluctantly made as she peered disgustedly at his huge, recumbent form.

With the open cutter out of action it fell to Catherine and Liz to ferry all the waiting passengers. The lengthy task completed, they returned to tow Mo's disabled boat back to the moorings for the rest of the night. The uninvited guest snored on oblivious.

"He can bloody well get himself out of it."

Mo voiced a final angry valediction. Although he was gone when she came down in the morning, he left his mark by two empty bottles and a splintered engine casing.

"I've had enough of Christmas to last several times round." Catherine whispered to Liz as they crept into their bunks, careful not to wake their cabin mates.

"Ditto," came the weary reply. "Just think Boxing Day's started already and we have to be on stage for the Knave tonight."

Catherine closed her eyes, willing the morning to keep away.

<u>Chapter Ten</u>

Catherine stood in the wings, seeking body warmth with the rest of the chorus. It was draughty and she was very cold. Her paper hat, resembling a jam tart, rustled in the breeze and her legs topped by navy knickers, regulation blackouts, were covered in goose pimples. She could hear Mo as the Knave, on stage, arguing in rhyming couplets with the King of Hearts something about having nookie with cookie. The King, a joiner from the Maintenance Yard chosen for his powerful voice and first class rendering of One Eyed Riley, lunged at Mo who danced off stage. The piano-accordion struck up the Can-Can, cue for the chorus to get on stage. Linking arms, in a ragged line, they took to the platform. Catherine, aware of massed faces beyond the footlights, was startled by catcalls and foot stamping as the audience responded to the tartlets' high kicks. She lost her hat but at least she was warm.

June, resting on Bill's bunk, wondered lazily how the Pantomime was progressing. Most of Bill's crew were at the show to cheer Martin in his part as Joker of the Royal House of Cards. Bill's Landing Craft was temporarily moored alongside the pontoon. There was some problem over berthing which Bill was to sort. In the meantime, June waited in a happy vacuum of anticipation for his return. The centre light of the cabin was switched off, but the photograph of Bill's wife and small son pinned to the bulkhead was still visible. June spoke to the woman in the picture.

"I ought to feel guilty. I'm not trying to take anything away from you but I'm here and you aren't."

She drew on her cigarette deeply.

"It's now that matters, there may never be a tomorrow. And, hell, I just want as much of him as he'll give. I've never wanted any man as much. If I choose to give myself freely and not expect any return, surely that's up to me."

But into her mind, unbidden, came a picture of her family, on the farm, playing Christmassy games and in particular her father's disapproving face. She shrugged, "Times have changed Dad, we're all growing up". She blew a nearly perfect smoke ring and thought of a wish.

Back at the Base, the curtain came down for the interval. The Cast collapsed in the changing room, congratulating each other they had survived so far.

"How can you look so cool and calm Liz?" Catherine's flushed face stared back from the cracked mirror.

"Truth is, I'm absolutely frozen."

Liz huddled in her duffle coat, looked more like a sick arctic explorer than the Princess of Universal Hearts.

"It's bloody freezing on stage, sitting there for ages, with that feeble bit of tapestry and having the Ace breathing beer and onions all over me."

She eyed Catherine enviously.

"I'd rather be you, leaping about in the chorus."

"Darlings, you are all wonderful."

Doug appeared waving a bottle.

"You've got the audience eating out of your sticky mitts."

He looked at his limp company of players and, remembering the flops in repertory, passed the bottle round.

"A swig can help keep out the cold and keep up the spirits."

"Brandy should make a good cocktail with beer and onions," Mo teased Liz and passed the bottle on to the King. "A spot of lubrication should boost the One eyed Riley."

"You were wonderful."

Pete, the co-producer, made time to praise Liz before rushing off to mend a foot light wrecked by the Joker's heavy tread in a clowning scene. The raucous sound of the Claxton announced the second half. Liz hastily swallowed Doug's fiery medicine, scorching her throat but not heating the rest of her body. Martyred to the cause, she flung off her duffle coat, snatched up the offending tapestry and hurried onto the stage.

June lay in Bill's arms, beyond thoughts of her father, the farm or the pantomime. Time stood still as she waited in expectation. Bill stroked her mass of sun bright hair, smoothing the waves back from her forehead.

"Let me love you properly, darling Juniper."

He used his pet name for her.

"I've wanted you for so long."

He gave her a long, lingering kiss and fumbled with the buttons of her shirt.

June felt as if she was in a dream, remote, unable to respond. The longed for moment had come. Her mother never spoke of it. Information had only come from school friends and procreation on the farm. The desired yet dreaded sexual intercourse. If only she had done it once before. It was agony to be so ignorant and without confidence. Then miraculously, her commonsense took over.

"Let me."

She sat up. Pushed Bill away quite roughly and finished unfastening her shirt. Bare skin to bare skin and her body became alive, like a finely tuned instrument, hyper sensitive to Bill's every touch.

"My sweet darling girl," he murmured as his hands and lips explored her responsive body. June rubbed the back of his neck and ran her fingers experimentally down his spine. She was pleased with his shivered reaction. His arms were strong and hard as he cradled her, cupping her breasts and moulding her nipples with his tongue. He led her gently forward, inexorably, with practised skill. The rhythm of movement increased and she gave herself to him, disintegrating and melting in the ecstasy of their union, until the sharp pain of reality told her she was no longer a virgin. She remained secure in his arms, tasting salt from her own tears. Curiously tired yet lapped in well being she drifted into a dreamless sleep.

June woke to find she was alone. A cup of tea and a scribbled note was on the shelf by the bunk, next to the ash tray and empty packet which had held Bill's precaution. The message read: Summoned by Q.M. to deal with problem on the Mess deck, shan't be long, Bill. June rubbed her eyes and re-read Bill's untidy scrawl. Her mouth was dry. The tea was cold. How long had she slept? She struggled into her clothes, hurrying them on anyhow, so great was the urge to escape, to a place where she belonged and felt comfortable.

The dimly lit passage was empty. June climbed the ladder leading to the deck. She heard distant voices but saw no one as she crossed the gangway onto the pontoon. Her bicycle was still propped against the wall. The saddle felt hard and uncomfortable, a salutary reminder of her recent experience.

Russets was quiet, most people were still at the Pantomime. June carried a mug of tea to the bathroom. She watched the steam rise from the hot water as the bath slowly filled. Lying in the comforting warmth, she heard distant noises of people returning to the quarters.

Mo's voice, "June, are you there?"

June wrapped a towel round her dripping body and opened the door. "Mo, I'm in here. Can you come?"

It sounded like a cry for help. Mo shut the door and leaned against it, waiting for June to tell her what was wrong.

"I've been with Bill," June said slowly. "I should be stupendously happy, so why am I all muddled and sad?"

Mo reached up and putting her arms round June, patted her reassuringly. "Tell me about it."

Her familiar freckled face and matter of fact tones steadied June. She felt calmer and ready to talk.

At the end of the production, Doug had arranged a stage party for the performers. Liz had the shivers and would not stay.

"If your skin feels prickly and tender, you are ill," Catherine advised.

Pete nodded, wanting to take care of her. "You'd better get to bed. Hang on to me and I'll see you to Pantiles."

Liz felt light headed and was glad of his arm but hoped he would not read too much into her sudden dependency. She leaned against him.

"Don't kiss me. You might catch what ever deadly disease I'm hatching."

Her closeness and the smell of her perfume made Pete close his eyes.

"Thanks for bringing me home."

She was gone. He was alone with his frustration outside Pantiles.

The second Catherine woke she was mindful of the silent bunk above.

"How are you?"

"Peculiar."

Liz's voice was harsh and several octaves lower than normal.

"I've got a hell of a throat, really hard to swallow but I'm so thirsty."

"Help, I'll get some water."

Catherine was alarmed for Liz and then for herself. If Liz was ill, how could she run the Cutter? Liz could only manage small sips. She refused breakfast and could not think of moving.

Mo and June were eating toast, heads bent in conversation. Catherine rushed in with her news ending with, "What should I do about her? She's really ill. Then there's the boat business to sort if I'm on my own."

"The duty wren will cope with the Liz part." Mo knew the answers. "As for not having a crew, that's really the Bosun's business, unless," she looked sideways at June who appeared to be caught up in a dream.

"Hey June." She jogged her arm, "As the Crash boat's on the slips, couldn't you or Maggie help Catherine out?"

June surfaced and brightened, "Maggie's on a weeks leave from tomorrow, but no reason why I can't join Catherine".

"That's a truly great idea, thanks." Catherine was delighted, swallowed a hasty breakfast and hurried off to put everything in motion.

Mo was also pleased with the plan. Much better, she thought, for June to help Catherine than moon over a paint pot on her own. Mo had pondered over June's reaction to Bill's attentions. She remembered, only too well, her own initiation behind the bicycle shed in that Welsh playground. Spotty Dave had won her on the rebound after months of not being loved or wanted by the Misses Jones. The memory of Dave's perspiring face pressed close and the shock of his wet kiss and protruding tongue was not a pleasant one. What followed through his insistence and her compliance had been happily superseded by more rewarding sexual adventures. Mo wondered if growing up in a sheltered family could have affected June's reaction.

Liz was admitted to the Sick Bay with a streptococcus infection. She lay in bed with a high temperature, drifting in and out of sleep, hardly aware of her surroundings. The last time she remembered such a sore throat was following a tonsillectomy performed on the dining room table. Aged six her convalescence at home had been relieved by ice cream fed by her father, stories read by her mother, comfort from Nanny called back to care for her and the gently hissing gas fire, casting an orange glow behind the high nursery fire guard.

Someone said, "She's over there in the bed by the window." There was the familiar quick footsteps clicking across the linoleum and a faint suggestion of muguet du bois. For a moment, Liz believed she was truly back in childhood. She opened her eyes. Her mother, poised and elegant, totally in command of the situation was standing there.

"Darling, you have been horridly ill." Liz had forgotten how distinctly her mother spoke, emphasising her words. "The Grand P's contacted me and then Tommy gave me a lift down. He had some sort of business with the Dean in Winchester, he has a small allowance of petrol for those sorts of journeys." She kissed Liz on the forehead and laid a sheath of roses on the locker. A nurse came forward with a chair, Liz's mother smiled and sank gracefully down, crossing one silk-stockinged leg carefully over the other.

"What a surprise," Liz croaked.

"Don't try and talk if it hurts, darling." Her mother held a finger to her lips.

"I won't stay long but I had to see how you are. It all sounded quite awful and the Grandparents practically ordered me to come."

She removed her small, close fitting hat and ran her fingers through thick dark hair, so like her daughter's but shorter and neater.

Liz eyed her mother critically, noticing new lines at the corners of her eyes and mouth. Otherwise she looked as ageless as ever. A cup of tea appeared, reminding Liz how her mother prompted service without making any request.

"I'd like you to meet Tommy, darling, but now is not the moment when you can't be at your best."

She stroked Liz's hand and gave an uncertain smile.

"You must come up to London, when you've quite recovered. You could bring your nice friend Catherine with you. And meet Tommy, I'm sure you will like him."

Liz nodded. She felt her mother needed reassurance. It was good of her to come when she was so busy with important work and now there was Tommy. Liz lay back on her pillows as her mother gaily waved from the door. She felt very tired and was pleased to be left alone. The photograph lying by the roses was of an older man leaning against a vintage Bentley. He wore a clerical collar.

"He's not the sort of boy friend I would have expected."

Liz passed Catherine the picture.

"What a super car."

Catherine perched on the side of the bed.

"Maybe that's the attraction, although he does look kind. Why do they have straps round their middles?" Liz stared and Catherine added, "I mean the car, silly."

Liz laughed until it hurt and began to feel better.

"Don't get too used to June, I'll be back sooner than you think."

"I'll be glad when you are. June refuses to take over as Cox but she's not much good on the engine, she's not a proper stoker like you. In fact she's been sort of odd, vague and dreamy, not her usual self at all. I wonder if she's in love."

"I bet that man Bill's something to do with it." Liz was cross.

"Why don't you like him?" Catherine challenged as she handed back Tommy's photograph.

"I think it's rotten for anyone to forget about a wife, alone at home left with all the responsibility of bringing up their child. War gives some people the opportunity to take what they want, regardless." Liz shook her head. "But hell, June's old enough to know the score." She changed the subject. "Is Chris back from leave?"

"Should be tomorrow. I promised, we'd spend an evening together at the Duck and Feather swapping our Christmas experience. He's bound to want to hear about the pantomime, so maybe Doug and Pete will come too. Pity you can't be there; Pete asks after you all the time."

Liz made a face. "He comes here regularly and leaves a trail of things to prove it." She frowned. "I wish he wasn't so keen, he's O.K. as a friend."

"He'd like to be more than that." Catherine pointed to a nurse advancing with carnations and Pete's latest message.

Liz raised herself in bed and said despairingly, "I don't want to get involved deeply with anyone. Pete's nice enough and I'd hate to hurt him. No one knows what's ahead or who will be there at the end of it. It's a bad time for him too, not knowing the future. Maybe he needs someone but I'm not the right person". She plucked at the sheet, pleating it mercilessly between her long fingers.

Catherine seeing her agitation, picked up the flowers.

"They ought to be in water. Shall I find a vase?"

Liz nodded gratefully, exhausted into silence after her outburst.

"You know, when you are quite well, we could go up to Town on a twenty four hour pass. Your mum wants you to meet Tommy and we might see Sam. He's up there, working on a project for his college course."

Liz smiled her approval.

June was not the best stoker but she compensated for her lack of engineering knowledge by teaching Catherine all she knew on seamanship. She was grateful for Catherine's company when facing Bill and his crew and gradually regained confidence. Bill was attentive towards her in company and loving when they were alone, but he went no further than the superficial bounds of necking. Boxing Day was not mentioned. June was mostly comfortable with the situation, preferring to avoid confrontation.

As time passed, she almost wondered if anything had happened. She was due for leave, but used the excuse the Farm would be dreary in the winter and she was needed on the river.

The river was cold and inhospitable. The girls on the boats suffered chapped hands from the constantly wet ropes and some developed chilblains. The Cutters were open to all weathers and duffle coats failed to keep out the icy north-east winds. The flotillas took pity on them when there was time to spare between trips.

"We drink so much tea; our insides must be a permanent rust colour," Catherine complained to Chris when warming up in his wardroom between night duty trips.

"Less lethal than gin," Chris advised. "I find too much spirits gives me indigestion. I'm better off on beer." He looked at her critically. "If you wear any more sweaters my arms won't be long enough to go round you. How about borrowing my sheep skin waistcoat?"

Journeys outside the river became hazardous. The sea was wild and hostile, whipped into steep waves by the merciless gale force winds. Stinging rain easily turned to hail, hurtful on exposed faces. Catherine learned from June to plan carefully in advance, take account of wind and tide and above all remain calm. The sight of June grinning under the brim of her sou'wester, fair hair escaping in wet strands, cheeks puce from the arctic wind, gave Catherine confidence.

Two weeks later and the Crash boat was ready to go in the water. Maggie was back from leave and June's time with Catherine was up.

"Can't teach you any more anyway," she told Catherine. "You are absolutely fine. It's only practice now and bully for you having Liz, the best stoker here."

She left without a backward look, already thinking ahead to the Crash boat and Maggie.

Liz was better and bored, longing to be back on the river.

"But first we'll go to London," Catherine persuaded. And Liz, curious to meet Tommy, despite herself, agreed.

Chapter Eleven

"Sam, listen, I'm running out of money. Liz and I will be in London on Saturday, where can we meet? About tea-time? Where did you say? Of course we can find it. Four o'clock then."

Catherine was cross. Did Sam think they were idiots? Did he really want to meet them? He sounded preoccupied, distant, not only geographically. She handed the telephone to Liz.

"It's engaged but I'll try once more." Liz eyed the queue of wrens behind them. Catherine saw her nod and start speaking, stop and nod again. She kept on nodding then held the receiver away from her ear. Catherine heard the staccato voice at the other end, speaking excitedly, swamping Liz with plans. Liz put down the phone.

"Just as well we're meeting Sam first. There won't be a moment to breathe after that."

Liz, discharged from the Sick Bay, waited at Pantiles. Catherine cycled up the tow path at top speed, changed working rig for uniform and, with Liz, tore down the road in time to catch the bus.

"Bloody hell, this time tomorrow we'll be back on the river having been to London, seen Sam, Tommy and your mother," Catherine panted as she climbed the stairs to the top of the bus.

The train was in. They sprinted through the barrier, waving travel warrants at the bemused ticket collector, left clutching a mixture of used tickets and in and out of date passes. Doors banged and the guard blew his whistle.

"Get in anywhere."

Liz frantically clawed at the nearest carriage door. It opened at her touch and large hands pulled them aboard as the train began to move.

"Knock me down if it ain't those sea going dames. Remember me and my buggy way back in the fall?"

Hank had rescued them for a second time.

"Move over and make space for my girls," the American commanded and shouldered his large frame fractionally closer to his neighbour.

Catherine held her breath and inserted herself into the crevice appearing to his left. Liz squeezed into the miniscule gap between shifting bodies on the opposite side. One of them with extreme difficulty extracted a packet of gum from his pocket.

"Spearmint?" he offered.

Liz leant across for Catherine to benefit. They settled down to chew their way to London. Hank's buddies were on weekend leave. Someone produced a pack of cards and a swift, hard selling poker game was organised.

"We're all set to do little old London Town. Care to join us at Rainbow Corner, our G.I. club, Piccadilly way?" The gum beneficiary eyed Liz appreciatively. "I'd sure fancy a jitter-bug with you, Ma'am."

"Just imagine your mother's face if we turned up with six Yanks," Catherine said as they waved goodbye at Waterloo.

"Funny bumping into Hank like that."

"He's larger than life, but you can't help liking him. Hang on to me, there's such a scrum and we don't want to get separated."

The station was packed with people, mainly in uniform.

"We'll take the Northern line to Leicester Square and walk through to Piccadilly, to save having to change. The tubes will be crammed at this time on a Saturday."

Liz knew London. The crowded underground platform showed no sign of nightly habitation. Air raids over London had eased since the onslaught of the blitz. A gust of cold air and a train exploded from the mouth of the tunnel to screech to a standstill. Doors slid open with extreme reluctance and everyone surged forward. Passengers wanting to leave jostled and shoved.

"Feels like I'm in a tide rip."

Catherine, hanging on to Liz, was miraculously in. She thought, "If someone died they'd still remain upright".

"Third stop," Liz reminded.

They fought to keep their place at each station. The lights flickered on and off and then, just short of Leicester Square, the train stopped.

"Please let it go on," Catherine sent an urgent request to a deity who might be tuned in. Awful to miss Sam and it was hard to breathe in the crush.

Someone shouted, "It's a long way to Tipperary".

And a joker added, "Farewell Leicester Square".

There was a general laugh and as if in denial the train eased forward into the station.

"A pip squeezed out of a lemon must feel like this."

Catherine checked through her belongings before following Liz up the stairs to ground level. The lifts were out of order. Emerging into thin winter sunshine, Catherine took huge gulps of air. Liz guided her from the Charing Cross Road through Coventry Street to Piccadilly, monopoly names to Catherine.

"So sad lovely Eros has gone," she said as she pointed to the empty space where the god of love had stood.

"Anyway," Liz pointed to the happy couples seated on the sandbags round the base of the boarded fountain, "You can see his influence is still around".

"There's Sam. Look Liz, to the left of the entrance to Lyons Corner House."

The tall, thin young man slouching against the portico of the restaurant, put his sketch-book in his jacket pocket and waved.

"Sam, we're here."

"Cat, I've got eyes. You are large as life and almost as beautiful."

He gave Catherine a hug and held out his hand to Liz.

"What shall we eat? One queue is for rabbit food and no doubt the other is for rabbit itself. But may be you're to feast tonight. I'm off to Brighton and home comforts, probably a fatted calf will be fitted in to my weekend."

"I suspect my mother will have arranged a sort of public fatted calf for us," Liz told Sam who raised his eyes in mock alarm. She hastily added, fitting in with Sam's banter, "My mother wants to take us out to celebrate this prodigals return".

"So, let us avoid queues and take tea somewhere else," Sam decided.

They drifted up Regent Street. Sam was in the middle with Catherine clinging to one arm while Sam caught hold of Liz's hand to include her. Both girls modified their pace to his slight limp. The coffee bar was half empty.

"Probably because they serve camp coffee, disgusting stuff," Liz prophesied.

She ordered a pot of tea in preference to which Sam added toast and jam. Over tea, Sam's chat kept them amused.

"The lodgings the College recommended near Kings Cross, is run by charming Mrs Green, no sign of Mr. This lady keeps her hair in curlers all day to look her best at night, in case she's bombed out. Or," Sam winked at Liz, "maybe she has hopes one of her lodgers will succumb."

"Likely to happen?" Liz mumbled, handicapped by a mouthful of toast.

"Not Pygmalion likely on her diet of corned beef in batter for firsts followed by Yorkshire pudding and custard."

Catherine listening to their exchange, dug into Sam's pocket for his sketch book.

"That's a lovely one of St Paul's, all that rubble round the base makes it look like phoenix rising from the ashes."

"So much that was good has gone." Sam was suddenly serious, "It'll take an age of sorting when the war is over".

Liz shivered.

Sam leaned towards her, looking into her eyes. "You've been ill, Cat told me. Are you really O.K. now?"

Liz was arrested by his question. She thought: Eyes are meant to be mirrors of the soul. Catching his solemnity, she replied, "Me? I'm well now. But, you know, being in bed gives you thinking time and I just hate knowing that more and more people and places will turn to ashes and dust before the violence stops".

Sam touched her hand lightly, where it rested on the table between them. Liz noticed the paint smudges on his knuckles. "There was a choice to let a madman run the world or to stand up and be counted. So in the end we had no choice. You, and Cat here, are lucky to be doing something about it actively." He glanced down at his left boot with the built up sole.

Liz, following the direction of his eyes, replied quickly, "But you, with your expertise, will have the more important role of rebuilding when the madness is over".

Catherine listened, pleased that Liz was concerned for Sam's loss, rather than her own. She did not add that buildings might be replaced but what about people?

Sam smiled at Liz, acknowledging her understanding.

"Don't look so serious Cat, you'll get frown lines." He was back to his teasing mode.

They said goodbye at the Circus entrance to the Underground.

"I won't come down. It's easy to catch a bus from here to Victoria and I hate tubes, so stuffy, and you see more of the world from the top of a bus."

He gave Catherine a hug.

"Remember us at home and don't let Cormorant take too many liberties."

Liz stood back considering the cousins. They did not look alike but had the same quirky sense of humour. Sam turned towards her and she held out her hand in farewell. He took it, gravely, and kissed the palm.

"Better than silver for a dark eyed gipsy of the sea. Wish me well and say we'll meet again."

Not waiting for a reply, he was soon lost to view in the pavement crowd.

Catherine shouted, "Give my love to Alex and Dad and to Mum." She laughed. "Same teasing old Sam. London hasn't changed him at all. I do love him. Which line is it for St John's Wood."

Liz followed her, wondering what sort of love Catherine meant. There were seats available on the Bakerloo line. Liz and Catherine sat in silence, absorbed in their own thoughts. Liz was tired and apprehensive. How would it be meeting Tommy? Could he possibly be a future step-father? No one could replace her father. Catherine mulled over the afternoon. She had wanted Sam and Liz to like each other and the meeting had worked. She wondered what the evening would hold. Mrs Howard sounded rather grand and what would Liz be like with Tommy?

St John's Wood streets were quiet and well bred. The trees were pruned and the gutters clean but mounds of rubble filled gaps between the fine houses. Mrs Howard had the use of a spacious house in a wide road. The owners had moved to the safety of the country and were delighted someone, they knew, was looking after their home.

Dusk had set in and the air was sharp and cold when they climbed the shallow steps and rang the bell. Mrs Howard flung open the front door, kissed both of them and swept them through the tiled hall, up the curved staircase to a double bedroom on the first floor.

"I'll leave you to freshen up, there's a bathroom across the way. Then come and join us in the small sitting room to the left of the front door. I don't use the big drawing room, that fire simply eats fuel." She paused to draw breath. "A taxi is ordered for seven thirty and it would be nice for you to meet Tommy and have a drink before we leave." She left the room with a swirl of her full skirt, leaving remnants of her scent behind.

"Where are we going? Oh dear I forgot the toothpaste." Catherine pulled her pyjamas and tooth-brush out of her gas mask case.

"She said she would book a table at the Trocadero. That's an eating place we used to go with Daddy, back in the West End. Liz frowned but offered mildly, "You can use my toothpaste. I'm going to look for the bathroom".

Catherine wandered round the room. There was a framed sampler in cross-stitch by Cissie and a picture of a small girl with long black hair holding a hoop.

"Are you Cissie?" Catherine asked.

Otherwise the twin beds with oak headboards, matching dressing-table, chest of drawers and wardrobe gave no clue to the owners' identity. Brushing hair, putting on fresh lipstick and examining precious silk stockings for flaws took only minutes. The door to the small sitting room stood open. Heavy curtains hung generously across the windows, lamps cast pools of light onto the richly patterned carpet and the polished surface of dark furniture reflected vague images.

Mrs Howard broke off her conversation and came forward, the man of the photograph, close behind her. He took Liz's hand in both of his and for the second time that day she was struck by the firm grip, although these hands were broad and capable unlike Sam's slender tools of trade.

"Liz darling, this is Tommy."

"Elizabeth," he said, savouring the name, "It is good to meet. Your mother has talked so much of you and the tragic time you've both been through. This awful war has so much sadness".

Liz looked up; he was only a little taller. His round cherubic face had crinkles round the eyes and his mouth turned up at the corners. He did not kiss her but held her hand gently in both of his, like holding a frightened bird.

He turned to Catherine, "I hope there'll be a chance to tell me about the boats and what you do, that's if it isn't too hush-hush." He smiled at Mrs Howard. "Margaret never tells me what she's up to. Would you both like a sherry?"

"It's very dull. I sit in an office most of the time. It's not nearly as glamorous as a boats crew wren." She sipped her drink and offered no further information.

"Now Tommy should tell you what he does, for he's a man of many parts."

"Well the sum of my parts will have to wait, as I think that's the taxi," Tommy said firmly, "and I'd better catch him as he won't be able to see the numbers in the blackout".

Catherine chose one of the flap-up seats in the taxi. Tommy sat in the middle of the back seat with Liz and her mother on either side. Liz, stiffly upright, turned away to stare out of the window. Her mother linked her arm with Tommy, resting her gloved hand on his worn overcoat sleeve.

The Trocadero was all red plush and gilt, very Victoriana. There was a steady hum of conversation and an appetising smell of food. Margaret Howard was known and the table booked.

"Essential on a Saturday," she explained.

Most of the diners were in uniform and some showed interest in Liz and Catherine's white lanyards.

"That's a new one on me," a Major remarked in passing, to a blonde A.T.S. in khaki. They missed her giggling reply.

The menu was imaginative and long, most of the main dishes were based on chicken or fish. Tommy and Catherine chose roast chicken.

"It's everything that goes with it that I like," she confided.

Liz and her mother ordered sole.

"Fresh up today," the waiter assured.

Before the food arrived, Tommy asked to be excused. He walked over to a table where a man, in R.A.F. uniform, sat with a diminutive girl in a green dress. Her tawny hair piled on the top of her head only added slightly to her stature. The man turned at Tommy's approach, his face was badly puckered and discoloured. Catherine drew in her breath; she found it difficult to look at the disfigurement.

"Part of Tommy's work is at East Grinstead. He goes every week to talk with the patients in Archie McIndoe's Burns Unit." Margaret Howard crumbled her bread. "He has enormous sympathy for anyone suffering scarring. I suppose it's not surprising. His wife and son were badly burned in 1940, when the fire bombs rained down on London." She examined the pile of crumbs she had made. "Poor Tommy, they didn't survive."

Two people whose lives had been shattered by the war. Catherine wondered: How did they meet? They are so different, Tommy round and ordinary and Liz's mother beautiful in a brittle, sophisticated sort of way. Both probably lonely, Tommy's lost a child but Mrs Howard still has a daughter.

The Waiter arrived with the chicken as Tommy rejoined them.

"It's Mac's first trial run up to Town. You know it takes a lot of courage facing crowds for the first time. Still, Vera a nurse from the unit, is with him. A toughie but great at easing the way."

"It's just an idea, but mightn't we ask some of the boys to St John's Wood?" Margaret Howard smiled at him." It could be a stepping stone towards facing the crowds."

Warning notes of the air raid siren sounded as they left the restaurant.

"We'll take the underground in preference to finding a taxi," Tommy counselled.

Other people had the same idea and the train when it eventually arrived was packed. The dark streets of St John's Wood were almost empty.

"Best get under cover," an air raid warden, cycling past, warned. But the cheering notes of the All Clear sounded as they reached home.

"Thank goodness." Tommy opened the front door. "You girls look all in and ready for a good night' sleep."

Catherine could not keep her eyes open. She left her clothes in an untidy heap and fell into bed. Burrowing under the sheets felt like sinking into a warm pit. She was just conscious of someone coming into the room and turning off the light. Liz and her mother's murmured voices did not prevent her falling instantly asleep.

Margaret Howard leaned over to kiss her daughter goodnight and was surprised by the arms that reached up, pulling her down in a spontaneous embrace. Liz felt closer to her mother than ever before. In her childhood her father had come first. The two women recognizing a common ground, clung to each other, linked by the past but on the threshold of the future.

Margaret Howard softly closed the bedroom door and joined Tommy in the kitchen. Kicking off her high-heeled shoes, she smoothed her skirt before sitting at the table. Tommy poured tea into two gold-rimmed cups. She was suddenly struck by the difference between him and her late husband. She closed her eyes to see Jim the athlete, his long lean body and muscular arms. She opened them to look across at the thick set, burly clergyman, thinning hair streaked with grey. The only similarity was in their eyes, so kind. She knew, with certainty, it was this kindness she had loved and trusted and could love again.

He was concerned to see her cheeks were wet and recent tears had smudged her mascara.

"It's been a lovely evening, my dearest dear, and you have a wonderful daughter."

She could only smile her agreement.

Tommy's Sundays were filled with church matters, but Mrs Howard insisted on seeing them off at Waterloo.

"Come again as soon as you can," she called as the train gathered speed.

"We will, we will," Liz leant out of the window, her words snatched away by an incoming train on the opposite platform. She watched the waving figure shrink and finally disappear.

Catherine sank back on the carriage seat. "It's been super and I loved every minute but I'd hate to live in London, such miles and miles of buildings. Do you know, I meant to ask Tommy about his car and I quite forgot?"

Liz pushed the window up and secured the leather strap. She sat down next to Catherine in the empty compartment. "I'm really glad you made me come and the odds are on, you'll be seeing Tommy again and maybe his car." She tossed her cap on the seat and ran her fingers through her hair. "Just look at that sky, so dark and stormy. It jolly well would be rotten weather for my return to the river."

The London excursion was after all a small diversion from normal life. Cormorant, the landing craft and their own boats waited for them. They belonged on the river and they were impatient to return.

Chapter Twelve

"The Brits and Yanks have landed at Anzio." An excited Mo chased after June. "It was on the news after I.T.M.A." Mo was an ardent fan of Tommy Handley.

"Is that south of Rome?" June's geography was hazy.

"Yeah, on the coast, on the Tyrrhenian side. Bet they'll be in Rome in no time."

"The Germans won't let them through without a struggle. The Allies have had to fight for every inch up from the toe of Italy," June objected.

"Would possession of Rome make a difference this end? It does feel as if everything is beginning to hot up."

A few days later, standing at the tiller of her boat, with Dick standing below in the well, Mo voiced her concern. "It feels like we're on some kind of roller coaster, brakes off, surging ever forward."

Dick looked up. He was constantly surprised that such an unorthodox, independent being held such magic for him. A conventional man, believing in traditional values, he was never certain how this small defiant girl would react. Perhaps it was the attraction of opposites. But he did know that he would like to look after her.

"Nothing short of a universal cease fire will change our course now." His grey eyes were serious. "The sooner we get on with it the better. The way ahead is across the channel and into Europe."

"Take me with you when you go," she laughed down at him. "You'd have room for a small one like me."

"No space for any extras and that includes the ship's mascot, Brer Rabbit. The crew won't be happy, but a landing is certainly no place for a rabbit."

"He can stay and keep me company."

Mo was shaken, despite herself, by a vision of an empty river, devoid of the flotillas. However it worked out, the river would not be the same.

The heat was on. Visits from the services top brass increased. Boat trips to other establishments revealed growing numbers of craft hidden away in surrounding creeks and small harbours. Cormorant's Landing Craft spent more time exercising out of the river, sharpening essential skills and improving team work for the imminent Western Offensive. The wren boats crew saw them away at first light, spent the day either working in the river or ferrying about the Solent. The flotillas' return demanded instant response from the duty boats. It was considered top priority to assist the Landing Craft back on their moorings and act as their liberty boats ship to shore. The shared mission bound all the personnel closer. Pride in a joint service kept everyone working at high pitch. The strain was immense and showed in tired faces and sometimes frayed tempers. Off duty, the solace was social contact and simple pleasures to be found in the immediate area.

Winter slid into spring. Evenings became lighter. Winds, still strong and blustery, had lost their cutting edge. Liz, without chilblains, was happier. Catherine returned Chris's fleece lined waistcoat.

On a lightening visit to Briar Cottage, Mo surprised her mother feeding an orphan lamb.

"Quite the country woman," she told June on her return to Russets.

"How were they up at the Farm? Did they lose any lambs?" June was still undecided to take leave, but her family was on her mind.

"Not sure exactly, but I don't think many." Mo, cross-legged on her bunk, was sewing a button on her bell-bottoms. "But listen how Tom has taken to the Farm, not surprising, Patty and the twins make such a fuss of him. He won't think much of town streets after all those animals. But Mum, well once a Londoner always, I suppose. She gets on well with your mum but she'll never get used to all that space and she's scared stiff of the bullocks." She stopped to break the cotton with her teeth.

"Borrow my scissors. Did you see my parents?"

"Only your dad for a moment when he came to see Mum about a couple of slates off the roof. But Mum says your mother's a bit thin, she thinks she does too much. Although she's not needed so much outside as there's a second land girl." Mo looked across. "Why don't you take some leave and see for yourself?"

"Maybe I will." June avoided Mo's eyes. "But then there's so much going on here."

"Well Bill won't run away, he's too busy himself. There, that should hold me together a bit longer. Sad part was I just missed James. It would have been fun to see him but I really went for Mum and Tom."

James wrote to June, unexpectedly as they did not usually correspond. He referred to his own home visit and meeting Mrs Baker and Tom.

"He says he'd like to see you again." June relayed to Mo. His postscript referring to their mother, nudged her conscience and she put in for leave. Unfortunately, she was too late.

Cormorant was sealed for the first time, in anticipation of D Day. No one was allowed to leave Base, all leave was frozen and telephone calls were refused. June was upset and near to tears.

"I know it's to keep everyone guessing what's going on but I hate not telling the family."

"It's no good fretting about something you can't change. They'll understand later. Surprise in this game is all important; at the least it'll save lives and might very well ensure success." Bill put his arm round her. "I've got some space this afternoon, shall we take the whaler out? The tide is full and with this breeze we could enjoy the river."

The wind nipped June's cheeks and she pulled her woolly hat over her ears. She enjoyed working the jib with Bill at the helm, controlling the main sheet. Water gurgled against the sides of the sturdy clinker built hull, the boat moved through the water, seeming alive.

"I like this, no engine noise and the boat is so light and responsive."

Thoughts of the Farm receded.

Catherine was also on the river. She was learning to scull.

"It's only a knack." Chris made it sound simple.

"But how did you learn? You must have been taught."

"I've always known, since I sailed with my Grandfather on the Broads. He put me in the dinghy with one oar and told me to get on with it."

"Well I'm too old for that." Catherine was firm. "You must come with me and let me see how you do it first. Then I'll have a go and you can watch me."

He moved the oar from side to side with a flick of his wrist. The boat travelled smoothly through the water. It looked easy.

"The oar keeps coming out of the hole," she moaned.

"It's O.K., keep going, you'll get it in a moment. No, I'm not going to help."

They drifted, helpless, with the tide and came up hard against a giant mooring buoy. Chris hung on to the rusty ring while Catherine lost her temper.

"Stupid, rotten old oar."

She flung it down and sat heavily on the middle thwart. She felt angry and out of sorts. Everything seemed to be moving so fast and she was frightened of losing the ships and their men. She felt the pricking of tears behind her eyes and knew she was being absurd. The gentle lap of water against the buoy and crying gulls fighting for scraps from the ships calmed her.

Catherine addressed the oar, "You are only a length of wood, there is no reason why on earth I can't make you work for me as you do for Chris."

She stole a shame faced look at Chris where he sat forward, arms raised in mock defence in case her anger included him. She laughed, despite herself.

He lowered his arms. "Oh Catherine, I do love you."

"Do you really?" She was serious. "How do I know that's for real? And not because of this blasted work up game that we're all caught in."

"Come here."

He reached out and pulled her towards him, letting go of the iron ring. They drifted slowly in the turning tide. The dinghy rocked gently.

"It is hard for you as it is for all of us. The only way is to hang on and trust the people in charge, have faith in the training and our allies and hope that the sum of the total will pull us through."

He cupped her face in his hands and stared deeply into her eyes.

"Most of all, Catherine, you need to hear what I am saying. I love you at this moment in time. You cannot know the future, none of us can, so just accept the present as it is."

"I will, I will," she cried out. "But help, we're going to hit another buoy."

Catherine reported to Liz. "It was hard but I learned to scull in the end." They were pyjama-clad, in Pantiles' galley, savouring mugs of cocoa. "Did you know they put bromide in sailors' cocoa to take away their urges?"

"If that's true it's either not successful or imagine how extra lethal they'd be without it," Liz giggled. "Perhaps I should lace Pete's drink with the stuff. Might save me lots of no's. But to be serious, I have to let him get away with a bit, life's so fraught just now. I was talking to one of the stewards at the White House, the one with fluffy blonde hair, whose parents live in Portsmouth. Well she went home by bus only a week ago and said Pompy, usually bursting at the seams with service men, was very quiet. Her cousin, who lives over the hill, told her camps have sprung up everywhere and the countryside is simply dripping with Army."

"And now we've had one practice seal, I wonder what will happen next?" Catherine shivered and remembering Chris's words added, "Anyway I'm sleepy, whatever tomorrow brings, let's get our heads down now".

There was no immediate obvious change. May offered an early taste of summer with warm winds and balmy days. Mo and Stephie actually tried going in the river. Stephie involuntarily, when she lost her footing on a mooring buoy and Mo, tempted by the warm air, went in her swimming costume. Catching her breath in the clutch of icy water, she spluttered. "Get me out of here, it's too early."

Catherine had remained on the surface, exploring shallow creeks and inlets with Chris, ostensibly to practise sculling but really to be together.

The Base was sealed for a second twenty-four hours. No hardship as the growing tension and increase in troop and ship movement made everyone prefer to stay close to the river. The Duck and Feather became even more popular. Normal custom, swollen by an influx of army, strained their supplies especially the beer.

"Feels like time as well as booze is running out," Liz remarked, joining Catherine by the wheel, as they left the river to refuel.

"It jolly well has run out. Just look at that." Catherine clutched Liz.

In all directions, as far as they could see, from shore line to shore line, a vast armada of ships rode at anchor.

"Where on earth have they come from?" There must be hundreds, and so close together." Liz could not believe her eyes.

"Covering the water like a carpet. Looks as if you could tread from ship to ship all the way across the Solent without getting your feet wet."

"This is no practice; it has to be for real." Liz stood with her hand on her heart.

Cormorant was sealed for the third time. This time the Wrens' quarters began to fill with a strange assortment of precious belongings, including ships' mascots. Captain's rounds ceased and the Quarters' Officer chose, wisely, not to investigate.

"If we take any more, the law of the jungle may be a problem." Liz eyed Sooty, a tom cat, drooling below a caged canary.

"Could be worse at Russets with Dick's rabbit and Bill's terrier," Catherine remembered.

That evening, clinging to Chris in the dark, on the jetty, Catherine was too choked to say much.

"Look after yourself. I love you." Chris gave her a last hug.

"Love you too. Come back soon."

He was going and she faced the future alone.

<u>Chapter Thirteen</u>

They waited in their boats at the end of the jetty. The day was bright and breezy, an improvement on recent stormy weather. Normal routine was shelved and all boats and crews were mustered for immediate business. The river had hummed with activity since daylight. They had ferried boxes and boxes of stores, ammunition and equipment to the Landing Craft, lying on their usual moorings, the centre of attention. Catherine knew, with certainty, she was living history.

"Well, that should be the last of the baby blimps." Liz pointed at Mo's cutter, a nodding barrage balloon secured to a thwart, motoring up river. She turned and pointed towards the tow path.

"Look, here they come."

A dense column of men in khaki marched steadily along the path. They moved relentlessly forward, past the sentry at the entrance to the Yard and onto the Hard by the Landing Craft Headquarters. With scarcely a pause or change of step, the double line merged into a single file at the start of the jetty. Boots loud on the wooden planking, a file of determined men, dressed for battle, demanding to be taken to the waiting ships.

French Commandos, the first customers, bearded and taciturn, with knives glinting in their belts. Clambering across to fill the outside boats, they communicated little amongst themselves and not at all to the wrens.

"Did you see that beefy looking man picking his teeth with the point of his ghastly knife?" Liz shuddered. "None of them looked too clean."

"Can't have been much fun fenced up in camps for the last few weeks." Catherine motioned towards their next passengers. "The next lot look a bit awesome."

The French Canadians, giants of men, joked and growled their appreciation when they saw the women.

"Don't you give 'em an inch." Stripey rolled his eyes heavenwards. "They've been behind barbed wire three whole weeks."

"My hat, no woman will be safe this side or t'other. Lucky I sewed on all my buttons." Mo stood by to take the first contingent.

"That's enough, can't take any more." Catherine watched the rising waterline.

Liz slipped the gear lever forward. "If you must spit, put it over the side and not in the bilges," she told a tough looking man with a bristly chin.

The Canadians scaled the sides of the Landing Craft with practised ease. The sailors waiting to care-take them across channel were dwarfed by their splendid physique.

The third Commando Unit, British, were smaller but wiry and muscular. They carried sheathed, dagger-like knives and had a concentrated, determined air. Climbing quietly into the cutter, they thanked Catherine for the ride. Some, so young, reminded her of Alex. She was selfishly pleased he was still at school and Sam protected by a disability.

Late morning saw the last of the passengers. Military Commanders and the Landing Craft skippers, fresh from a final briefing, stood chatting, waiting to join troops and crews aboard the ships. The mood was light, exchanged jokes and laughter snatched away by the lively wind. Liz remarked, "Anyone would think they were off on a holiday excursion instead of to who knows what".

Pete, sailing as an extra Flags, stood close to Liz in the crowded cutter. He managed to squeeze her hand when she passed him his bulging brief case and she gave him a special smile as he scrambled aboard the Flotilla Leader. Chris waved to Catherine when she delivered his Commanding Officer Jim back on board, not the time for serious farewells.

It was strange returning to the jetty with empty boats. June's eyes were pink and she said sadly, "We are no longer needed".

"We've done what we can." Mo shrugged and made a face. "It's up to them now."

Flags fluttered bravely in the wind, crews lined the forecastle of each craft and music blared forth from loud hailers. Each skipper stood proudly on his bridge, right hand held in a farewell salute. Many times the flotillas had foamed out of the river but today differed. This was not a practice, they were leaving on the planned enterprise.

Empty of ships, the river looked strangely wide, but filled again almost immediately as a long line of small landing craft appeared from up river.

"They are so tiny to be going that far." Catherine waved frantically.

"Good luck to them." Liz gave the thumbs up sign.

The river was empty. All the landing craft, large and small, had gone.

Captain Morgan called Red to go with him to the river and see what was happening. Down through the trees and onto the reed beds. The reeds swayed from the ripples thrown up by the passing boats.

"That's it, my fine fella. They're on their way at last."

He addressed the dog snuffling in the mud.

"Damn my age, wish I could be with them. Bet that Catherine girl's busy." He shook his stick at Red. "You are filthy. Mrs Mim won't like you in her kitchen."

The setter eyed his master and shook himself free of the mud. They laboriously climbed back up the hill together.

Catherine realised how tired and hungry she was when she reached Pantiles. Wandering aimlessly into her cabin, she rubbed her hand over Chris's great-coat stuffed in the wardrobe. She discovered a slab of American compo-pact chocolate, ate greedily and then felt violently sick.

"The Allies entered Rome on the fourth." Liz, hoping for news had tuned in the wireless.

Catherine was restless and wandered over to the Whitehouse. She found June collecting scraps from the galley for Blighter.

"How soon will we hear?"

"Shouldn't think there'd be anything tonight. It's lucky for Blighter there are so many fussy eaters." She parcelled up the pieces of meat gristle. "I hope he'll eat this muck." June's concentration was on the ship's dog.

Catherine climbed wearily into her bunk. "I can feel the emptiness of the river from here."

Liz, above, was already asleep.

"Wake up. It's nearly news time." Liz climbed down over Catherine.

Anxious wrens in pyjamas surrounded the wireless.

"This is the seven o'clock news, our Allies have landed in France!"

It was the sixth of June, D Day. The longed for offensive into Europe had begun.

At breakfast, in the Whitehouse, it was the only topic of conversation. The news broke the suffocating silence, in existence since the ships' departure. The Base was unsealed as the secret was out.

Liz and Catherine cycled along the tow path towards the mouth of the river. The morning was overcast. The Solent, a metallic grey space, was empty of shipping. Wheeling gulls mocked.

"Well I had to be sure," Catherine said defensively, "that it isn't a dream.

That the whole lot has gone".

She turned her bicycle.

"Race you back. Not much time to change and get down on duty. But I can't imagine what the hell there is to do with no one to do anything for."

The Boat Officer planned to see departing and arriving watches together.

"All boat screw are on standby until further notice."

He scanned the listening group. "Duties on watch will continue as usual. Because you may be needed at any time there will be no shore leave until I give the word." He forestalled the inevitable questions. "No one knows what will happen and just because the flotillas have left," he paused, "temporarily, it does not mean you can have a holiday. We will use this time to tidy up the place and do everything we haven't had time to get done before."

"And he means we, which is he, too." Mo was ungrammatical as she took note of his oldest uniform.

The Boat Officer recognised he had a load of women to keep busy. He allowed no time for them to gloom over absent boy friends. He had them sorting the river, improving boat handling and seamanship. This work involved maintenance of catamarans, renewing wire pennants on the big mooring buoys and towing boats in and out of the Yard. He used the time as an opportunity to repair and renovate the fleet of duty boats. He made them feel they were preparing for a future when they would be needed. He tried to replace the mission which the ships had taken, with a new one - to be ready for their return. Despite the punishing work routine and new focus, the wrens' eyes continually turned to the river entrance, hoping to see the familiar square hulk of a returning landing craft.

Rumours began, some alarming and others contradictory. Talk of a particular ship sunk with no survivors, then it was not that one but another.

"I'm not going to listen anymore," Catherine declared.

"How much longer before there's anything definite?" Liz asked, waiting in the Q.M.'s hut for the few passengers that still used the duty trip across the river.

Stripey pointed towards the Hard. "Might be some news among that lot."

Liz followed his eyes to a dishevelled group standing outside the Headquarters. The men wore an odd assortment of clothing, some quite ragged.

"Who on earth?" Then recognition clicked into place. "It's some of Doug's crew!"

"Must run to time, can't keep passengers waiting, news will have to wait." Stripey was firm so Catherine and Liz had no choice but proceed on the duty trip.

However, one of their passengers, a wren writer from Headquarters had a tale to tell.

"Those poor men thumbed a lift on a supply ship, ending up at Portsmouth and had to make the rest of the way here by road."

"What happened to their ship?" Catherine was anxious.

"It struck an obstruction going in to the beaches and was grounded, completely out of action." The wren writer was factual, without emotion.

"What happened to Doug? He's the skipper." Catherine's eyes were wide and her body a question mark.

"They said he was very angry and last seen swimming towards the beach, carrying a tommy gun." The small, neat secretary adjusted her cap's chinstrap. "It's quite breezy out here."

Catherine laughed. "That's Doug all right, he'd be so frustrated."

Liz nodded, "Drama all the way. Theatre's in his blood, only this time instead of staying in production he's taken a star part."

"Thanks for the lift. Is he your boy friend?" The small wren climbed carefully onto the slippery catamaran.

"Not specially, but we like him a lot.

Catherine felt inadequate standing by the tiller in worn trousers and shirt, stained from scrubbing out. She could not explain the peculiar bond between the flotilla men and themselves. She was in a hurry to return to the Jetty and meet Doug's crew. But they had moved on, scooped up by the system to be recycled elsewhere.

Mo had caught them on the point of departure and relayed their memories of Operation Overlord.

"The coast sounds in a turmoil, disabled craft everywhere, some torn apart by underwater mines, others stuck on obstructions. Difficult to see what's happening through the smoke but masses of men, armoured vehicles and tanks seemed to be on the beaches. And the noise of aircraft, mortar and shell fire shattering." Mo added sadly, "They said lots of the little landing craft never arrived, because of the rough weather which was still around even though the operation had been delayed twenty-four hours".

Catherine ached for the brave little boats, waved away so cheerily by herself and Liz.

The Sick Bay, transformed into a minor reception centre, linked up with a clearing hospital some miles inland. The medical staff were on permanent standby for expected casualties. A trickle of ships began to appear in the Solent. Supply ships restocking with stores for the assault forces across the channel. Tankers refuelling to supplement Pluto, the pipe line under the ocean. Hospital ships, carrying wounded and sometimes dead personnel.

Open cutters were versatile, solid, stable boats with ample room for people and stretchers. Late one evening Catherine and Liz returned from supper to find Stripey on the telephone in his hut.

"Yes sir......yes sir......yes sir." He replaced the receiver. "They want you to help get them off. Can't tell you exactly what to expect but a Doc will be at the Pier Head this end. It's really a ferrying job."

The river was soft and mysterious in the fading light. Sea grass meadows merged with a shadowy shore-line. They passed the spit buoy wondering what was ahead. The converted hospital ship lay a short way out. A dark figure beckoned from the deck and Catherine secured alongside. Several people climbed down into the cutter and helped others behind them. Two stretchers were carefully lowered and then two long bundles.

"O.K. Jenny wren that's your quota." The officer on the deck above signalled them away. A white faced soldier helped gather in the bow line.

Clear of the ship's shadow, Catherine looked over her passengers. She was startled to see the women. A girl in a torn battle dress top held a bundle close to her. The bundle gave a cry like a sick bird and the girl wearily lifted a baby to her shoulder. An old woman, fingering a rosary, crouched by the engine casing. Liz moved among them reassuringly. Another girl spat at her.

"They was caught up in the Landing and not too 'appy to see us neither," the white faced soldier explained. "An awful lot of casualties, these two should make it O.K." He indicated the stretchers. "They're the unlucky ones," he said, pointing to the long bundles, "but at least they won't hurt any more."

Catherine refused to allow her mind's picture of Chris wounded or even worse, a bundle in her bilges. It was dark coming to the Pier head but the ambulances were waiting with the medical team. She felt profound relief at being no longer in charge.

Liz helped the old lady up the steps. "Suppose it had been my Gran," she said, eyes full of pain, later.

They all became used to meeting hospital ships and ferrying casualties but that was the only occasion French civilians were amongst them.

Chapter Fourteen

Dick's entire concentration was centred on getting his crippled landing craft back to the Maintenance Yard. The vessel was a sorry sight with a pronounced list to port, stanchions hanging and part of the bridge shot away. The exhausted crew, having survived the Landing and long return journey, entering the river was like coming home. Dick knew, despite the battering, they had been lucky. Injury to his crew was minimal and the craft still mobile. The initial briefing gave no expectation for their return, but he obstinately resolved to keep craft and crew serviceable as a personal contribution to the Western Offensive. His quiet determination was inspirational and enabled the crew to nurse their sick ship back to base.

Mo, with a leap of her heart, recognised the number on the side of the landing craft. She urged her cutter through the water to be the first. Stephie stood in the bows, straining her eyes to see who was on deck. Catherine, in the second duty boat, allowed Mo to forge ahead, turn in a wide sweep and keep pace alongside the disabled craft. In case more help was needed, she stayed astern. The Yard was prepared, maintenance teams impatient to start work on the first casualty.

Dick made his report to H.Q., checked his first lieutenant and crew were settled comfortably up at the Base and then looked for Mo. He found her in the garden at Russets talking to the rabbit. Mo, small as she was, stretched her arms around him. They sat on the low wall of the back garden. He could not find words and felt in his pocket for the envelope addressed to Catherine.

"Yes, Chris is O.K.," Dick replied to Mo's unspoken question. "He gave me this before we left the other side."

Mo thought of June. "Did Bill send anything for June?"

Dick bit his lip and his eyes clouded. He took both her hands in his, small like a child's, but rough and calloused as a workman. He held onto her for strength and when he found his voice it was flat and toneless.

Rotten business, Bill's ship was one of our first casualties." He closed his eyes to remember. "I was behind him, making for the beaches. It was rough and there was a lot of noise and smoke but the number on his stern was visible. One moment the ship was there and then it was pieces, falling all around. They must have struck a mine which blew them right out of the water, catapulting the crew into a sea of burning oil."

He shuddered at the memory of screaming men struggling in the cruel water. He opened his eyes to supplant the image but it remained vividly in his mind.

"Dick." Mo's voice jerked him back to the present. He forced himself to concentrate on the pattern made by the afternoon sun filtering through the trees onto the grass. The hideous image receded.

She spoke again. "Were there any survivors?"

He shook his head. "The ones picked up were too badly injured, except for Bill and he was horribly burnt, so goodness knows."

Mo crouched on the wall and wrapped her arms tightly round herself as if for protection. She felt cold in spite of the heat of the sun.

"June doesn't know. We must tell her together. Because you were there and I must be here for her."

They watched a bee poking a foxglove trumpet, searching for pollen, a steady munching came from the rabbit's hutch, ordinary happenings at an extraordinary time.

Mo stood up. "Come on, she mustn't hear from anyone else. She loves that ship and everyone and of course Bill most of all."

Mo found June in the cabin, listening to Edith Pfath singing Rien de Rein on her wind-up gramophone and brushing a protesting Blighter. People were about so Mo took June to where Dick waited in the garden.

Mo reached for June's hand while Dick told her. June said nothing but her normally high colour drained, leaving her face white and pinched. Mo felt June's hand clench inside her own. She could say nothing, words were useless.

Dick kept to practicalities. "He will have been taken to a hospital ship then to England to a large hospital able to treat burns." He did not say, his wife will have been informed.

June spoke at last. "Can you find out for me where he is?" She was calm and controlled.

"Of course." Dick smiled and lightly kissing them both on their cheek, left the garden to June and Mo.

Blighter pawed June for attention. She gathered his pliant body in her arms, feeling the living warmth through his fur. Mo sat on the grass, close, as June rocked backwards and forwards. They cried together for the men they had known and the ship June had loved. She hid from Bill's injuries, telling Mo, "At least he is alive and Dick will find out more."

Catherine and Liz were shocked. "After that Christmas we shared, I can't believe what's happened."

"Not to see Smithy, James or any of the crew again. So many at once is so awful." Liz thought of their families. Would Smithy's sister look after his Labrador?

Catherine slept with Chris's scribbled words of love and reassurance under her pillow. The knowledge of his survival coloured her days and filled her dreams.

Dick was the first but others followed, limping home for repair. News and letters came with them. The cutters met the most damaged craft to escort them through the Solent. The wrens secured their boats either side of the stricken craft, acting as surrogate port and starboard engines. The Yard maintenance crews worked elastic schedules, repairing maimed landing craft for the journey back to Normandy with precious supplies for the invading army.

Pete returned when his part in the operation was finished.

"He is quieter, not so persistent and there are grey bits in his hair." Liz told Catherine.

They were on their way to the strawberry fields, abundant with fruit. A ship was leaving and they fancied sending a basket. Catherine hoped some might reach Chris.

Turning out of Pantiles, they heard the harsh irregularity of an approaching engine.

"Funny noise for a motor bike." Liz wobbled over to the side.

The noise stopped and some one yelled from behind.

"Get down! In the ditch! It's about to explode." They all fell together, in a heap, a jumble of arms, legs, bicycles, dead leaves and brambles.

"What the hell?" Catherine demanded from under the stout frame of the Petty Officer wren from Pantiles.

P.O. Pam picked herself up and collected her tricorn hat from the centre of the road. "That must be a doodle bug." She looked at their blank faces. "You know, a flying bomb, like they are having over London, sort of pilotless aeroplanes. It's O.K. as long as you hear the engine, when it cuts out you must get under cover because that means it's coming down."

"I wonder where it landed?" Catherine removed a bramble. "It sounded close."

The first flying bomb in the area was an unpleasant surprise. Passengers in the duty boat sought for an explanation.

"Just a loner like that. Can't think why it came, after all it was wide of any service installation."

"Could have been to test distances."

"Maybe they were hoping for the Base or the Yard. That would put the kibosh on our work, patching up the flotillas."

Someone laughed. "In that case Gerry got his left and right muddled as it ended up the wrong side of the river."

"Do you know where it actually landed?" Liz asked a chippy from the Yard.

"Elsie, in the Duck and Feather, said somewhere in the woods. Fred Fosset, air raid warden, was checking but she didn't know if there was any damage."

Catherine watched the passengers disembark. "Captain Morgan walks Red in the woods. I hope he's all right. I think I might go over, time I paid him a visit anyway."

"I wish I could go with you but I promised to cover an extra afternoon for a stoker on the opposite watch." Liz sensed Catherine's anxiety. "It's a bit of a marathon on your own."

"Oh it's easy enough this time of the year. I'll go directly we come off watch, half tide then and the Q.M. will help me this end with my bike and no trouble the other side."

Catherine was glad of her sweater, there was a light wind off the sea. The wren coxswain sniffed the air like a hound on scent. "Could bring a sea mist later. What time are you returning?"

"Shan't be late, Liz and I are going to the film up at Base. It's Lady Hamilton, have you seen it?"

"It's great, Laurence Olivier's such a dish. Have a good ride, maybe see you later."

After the steep rise from the Duck and Feather, the going was easy. Catherine enjoyed pedalling along the twisting lane, peering over the hedges at the cultivated fields. It was good to be on her own and not lonely.

A lorry was parked across the lane, before the last bend to the cottage.

Catherine dismounted and inched round. She rubbed her eyes in disbelief. The gate opening onto the brick path, was the same, but little else. She let her bicycle fall anywhere as she registered the scene.

A man in A.R.P. uniform picked his way through the rubble of what had once been Captain Morgan's home.

"Proper mess, damned buzz bomb." He wiped the dust from his horn-rimmed spectacles. "Sad it had to be the cottage when there's so much space around." He replaced his glasses and looked at her, hanging onto the gate, bicycle lying on the ground. "Did you know the old chap then?"

Catherine nodded. She could not find breath to answer. The man sat her down on the brick path and pushed her head between her knees. Gradually the black spots receded as blood pumped back into her head.

He talked gently, all the while. "The old man and his dog were in the garden and killed outright. But his lady helper was still breathing when they dug her out. She's in hospital," he said comfortingly, "Shouldn't think the old fellow knew what had hit him, dog neither. Not a bad way to go, they were both getting on a bit."

"They still enjoyed life," Catherine objected. She walked round what was left of the garden, touching his plants. The scent of roses hung heavily. She longed for Chris and felt sick and alone.

The workmen gave her a lift back to the village, slinging her bicycle into the back to rattle with spades and pick axes. The men's voices rumbled above her, slumped between them. The earthy smell from their clothing penetrated her dream like state. Mist was beginning to gather in hollows and wreathe round the tops of trees, adding to the unreality.

They left her at the top of the hill, leading down to the Hard. She pushed her bicycle, too shaken to ride, past the Public House due to open in half an hour and down the alley to the catamarans. She waited silently for the duty boat, not seeing the river, running smoothly with smoky mist trails rolling in from the sea. In her mind, she walked in Captain Morgan's cottage, smelling his pipe tobacco and smoothing Red's warm head. She could not believe they only existed in her memory.

The cutter nosed slowly down river into thickening mist, the jetty appearing suddenly through the white curtain. Catherine was less wobbly but cycled slowly, only able to see a few feet ahead. Pantiles loomed, square and solid. She propped her bicycle against the coal bunker with the others. The back door gave at first touch.

"Thank goodness you're back." Liz, pink and excited, pulled her across the threshold. "I thought you'd never come. They're in. He's back!"

"Who? Chris? Where? Here?" Catherine was jerked into the present.

"For heaven's sake of course. Who else? And he's been looking for you." Liz spun her round quite roughly. "He's gone down by the road because we thought you'd come that way now the mist is so thick."

"I must find him." Catherine was furious with herself for not checking returning landing craft and the whiteout had covered what she might have seen.

"Go on foot, you might run him down on your bike." Liz laughed.

Catherine's breath rasped as she ran down the road. Chris turned when he heard her flying footsteps and just had time to hold out his arms before he took the full weight of her body. They clung, two figures melting into one, hidden from the world by the enveloping thick atmosphere.

"I thought I'd never find you." Chris held her close.

"I wanted you so badly, and you came." Catherine told him of the flying bomb and the tragedy the other side of the river.

Chris listened as they walked no where in particular, entwined, in step and perfectly in tune. Suddenly the church clock chimed.

"Help, the front door will be locked. I hope Liz has ticked me in and will unlock the French windows." Catherine cautioned, "Or I'll be in trouble."

Chris reluctantly let her go and watched from the road as she made a successful entry.

Liz closed and locked the French windows. "You missed a super film, but shouldn't think that worries you."

"So much to tell, it's been one hell of a day." Catherine yawned.

"Let it keep for tomorrow." Liz was tired and emphatic as she climbed back into her bunk.

<u>Chapter Fifteen</u>

June waited, wondering how to phrase the request. It was important to explain enough but not too much.

"First Officer Hemming will see you now. Just knock first," the wren clerk advised.

An appointment with Ma'am was serious, reminiscent of visiting one's headmistress. June stood in front of the massive desk, covered with neat piles of paper, a container for pens and pencils, a silver inkwell and matching ashtray. Her carefully planned speech faded as she waited for permission to speak.

First Officer Hemming, a small woman with neatly brushed lint coloured hair, came round her desk and led June over to the wide window, looking towards the river. She indicated for June to join her on the window seat and smiled encouragingly. Hemmy, as she was known by her contemporaries, had run a girls' reformatory before the war and had the reputation of a disciplinarian. She was also a frustrated mother who genuinely cared for the young women under her command; a quiet, controlled woman familiar with the happenings in her kingdom.

"You work on the boats, I believe."

"Yes ma'am." June relaxed, Hemmy knew of her. "It's the dog. He was only meant to be with me for a little, but he can't go back now." She hurried on. "May he stay with me at Russets till leave is allowed? Then I could take him home. My parents have a farm and he'd be all right there."

Jane Hemming listened quietly. She knew how involved her wrens were with the landing craft, particularly the girls working on the boats. This girl was one of them.

"Rules and regulations are essential in an organisation, but times of emergency call for a flexible approach." She spoke as June's First Officer. "Our flotillas have done a splendid job, sadly not without cost." She sensed the reason for June's underlying agitation. "It has been so important to back them up in many ways." Her sharp, grey eyes twinkled. "I am aware of the influx of livestock in the quarters. No doubt some of the less demanding may be absorbed but a young dog is another matter. Your terrier needs space, attention and no doubt training. However, I do understand the problem and he may stay temporarily, until the restriction on leave is lifted."

"When do you think that will be?" June had another problem to solve. "As well as taking Blighter home, I would very much like to see a friend who is in hospital." She hesitated and then could not help herself. "He is pretty sick."

"Friendship is very important to us." Jane Hemming chose her words carefully. "Probably your friend will have concerned family to visit him, especially if he is badly injured." She noticed June twisting her hands together. "You know it is natural to get very involved with a person at times of stress. Unfortunately it is more complicated when ill befalls them, then it is natural for relatives to give support. Friends can sometimes find themselves in a difficult position." She stood up, wondering if she had said too much. "On the question of leave, restrictions are about to be lifted but only to destinations within a radius of seventy miles, that is in case of a recall."

"She was really nice and understanding." June waited with Mo and Liz in the fortnightly line up for pay. "Leave will, any moment, be granted up to seventy miles."

"Mum will be worrying over Gina and the doodle bugs so I want to see her. Shall I take Blighter to the Farm?" Mo offered. "That'd save you some leave, but it won't solve how you are going to get to East Grinstead, that's over seventy miles."

"I'll fudge it somehow because I must go, and great if you would take Blighter."

"If Bill is in the Burns Unit at the Victoria, there might be a way Tommy could help." Liz signed for Catherine's pay. Chris's ship was off the slips and preparing to leave.

"St John's Wood must be within seventy miles and my mother would, I know, offer you a bed, no problem." Liz, although she had never liked Bill, was sympathetic to June. "And Tommy might be just the person to fix East Grinstead."

Margaret Howard was delighted to help. Liz so rarely asked for anything. Tommy was more thoughtful. "Of course I'm happy to take a friend of Liz with me, but hospital rules are very strict over visiting. If this man is severely injured, only close relatives will be allowed to see him."

"Darling, you know them all so well at the Victoria, I'm sure it will be all right. It could be vital for the man's recovery to see June." Margaret Howard's affection for Tommy, forged a bond with all women in love.

"I'll see what I can do." Tommy could not deny this woman, though he added sagely, "At least a visit could clarify the situation for June. Any chance of Liz coming up for a spot of leave?"

Requests for leave, following the restriction, were subject to a waiting list. Blighter was a nuisance. On duty with June, he barked incessantly and guarded the Crash boat as her personal property. Because of complaints, Mo was granted early leave to escort the dog to the farm. June put in for three days, destination London. Catherine and Liz did not ask for leave. The duty boats could be short handed and Chris was on the point of leaving.

London had become the prime target for Hitler's latest weapon, the V.1, a flying bomb. The public ridiculed its deadly action by using nicknames, buzz bomb or doodlebug. Anti-aircraft guns were transferred from the outer London barrage defence to the coast, backed by Spitfires they set out to destroy Germany's innovative weapon. Unfortunately, London became under siege once more. Those concerned for their safety again moved to the country.

June travelled alone to London. She was very happy to visit Bill but anxious. His burns were severe, how badly was he disfigured and did he want to see her? The reality of his wife lurked in the back of her mind.

She hurried up the steps of the Underground. A warning was on and there were few people about. "Can you direct me?" June showed the address to an Air Raid Warden, busily checking the sandbags round his post.

"Not far now." He peered from under his tin hat. "Don't forget, if you hear a blessed doodle cut out, dive for cover."

June listened. All she heard was sound of distant traffic, the clatter of a dustbin, a blackbird's song. She turned into Mrs Howard's road, as a ginger cat appeared and purred round her legs. June wondered how the farm cats would take to a new terrier.

Blighter cowered close to Mo. The train alarmed him, fear turning to aggression if anyone approached. Mo hung onto him tightly, he was awkward, her lap was slippery and her arms ached. The empty farm truck waited outside the station. Mo expected to see Mr Miller, June's father, but it was James who appeared from the Station Master's office, carrying a bulky parcel.

"Hi there, had to fetch this blade for the thresher. Dad's been going spare with so much work on hand. Is this the wicked Blighter?" Mo remembered June's brother from their previous meeting. He pushed her up into the cab, dog and bag behind the seats. "Training starts right here." He eyed the terrier and Blighter obediently folded his front paws over Mo's bag and remained quiet.

"What it is to have power of command." Mo mocked, silently approving. "How can the Fleet Air Arm survive without you?"

"Even star performers are entitled to leave." James put his foot hard on the accelerator, the ancient truck rattled and groaned along the twisting lanes. "Actually it's as well I came. One of the land girls is off sick, pregnant, and Mum's not so good. Your mother's been fab helping out. There she is, waiting for you." James screeched to a halt, leapt out and swung Mo down into her mother's waiting arms. Tiny folk, he thought, but both packed with energy and determination. "Steady old chap," he restrained the terrier, "You're coming home with me."

Mo only had a short time with her mother and scarcely saw Tom who was on the farm as much as possible. "It's good for Tom having so many of the Miller family around and he loves helping with the animals." Her mother unfastened her knot of red hair, streaked with grey, on her way to bed.

Mo picked up her father's photograph, as always, by her mother's bed. "Tom would have no memories of Dad's beastliness. I wonder where he is after all this time."

Mrs Baker put down her brush to rummage in the top drawer. She passed Mo an officially headed letter. "He's a prisoner of war in Germany. I received this notification a month or two back. It was forwarded from London. It must be terrible for him boxed up, he used to go mad if he were shut away."

"Oh Mum, how can you be sorry for him after all he did to you, when Gina and I were little and look how he left us all flat when Tom was a baby." Mo was exasperated.

"Of course I know all that, dear. But war changes folk and what we think about things. I don't hold malice, life's too precious with so much dying." She lifted her chin with determination. "Anyway I've written, just to help him through the long days. Probably won't hear back but there, I've done what I can."

"Oh Mum." Mo hugged her mother before going to her own room. She looked out, from under the eaves of the cottage, over moonlit fields. She did not want to see her father again.

A dark figure moved across the orchard, directly below the window. "It's magic, little Mo, come and join me," James called up softly.

Mo crept past sleeping Tom's door, left ajar and the bar of light under her mother's closed one. She slid back the bolt of the back door, feeling like an escaped prisoner. James took her hand and they ran, laughing, over the wet grass, in and out the shadows cast by the old apple trees.

"It's the only way we'll get a moment to ourselves. There are too many people and too much to do." James questioned, "Do you feel the same?"

Mo thought she did. For the first time she was in no hurry to return to the river. When the time came, James drove her to Salisbury. The petrol ration was easier and Mr Miller liked June's redheaded friend. He approved of Mrs Baker, standing up to him in support of his wife in her illness. Mo was like her mother but more amusing, and like his son, he enjoyed her teasing manner. James and Mo kissed as she boarded the train.

"This is not a good bye," James whispered and Mo understood.

Mo heard the duty wren lock the front door as she signed in. She was surprised by June's signature on the line above; she was not expected until the following day. June was in their cabin getting ready for bed. She pulled on her dressing gown and led the way back to the kitchen.

"Glad you're both in." The duty wren put her head round the door. "Don't forget to turn off the lights. I'm off for a bit of shut eye."

"How was it?" June asked about her family, the farm and Blighter settling down.

"Tell me how it was for you?" Mo sensed June's narrative would take time and she lit the gas under the kettle to make tea.

"Mrs Howard's Tommy took me by train to East Grinstead and then it was hospital transport. He seemed to know everyone and got me a cup of tea in the waiting area while he disappeared to make enquiries." June remembered her impatience at the delay. "An older man and woman were talking quietly, I couldn't hear what they were saying. The woman looked tired and sort of dispirited. Then a younger woman came and joined them, and, oh Mo, it was the girl in the photo, Bill's wife."

Mo did not interrupt.

"The man offered his seat but she stood, leaning over the sad woman. I felt like hiding although they did not know me or where I was from. Bill's wife spoke and I listened. She said, 'I think he really is a little better at last. At least he knew I was there and gave my hand the smallest squeeze. It was so wonderful to have that tiny reaction after sitting by him for so long with nothing.'"

June sighed. "You know she is fair, like me, much prettier than the picture. Bill's wife put her arm round the older woman; she said something I couldn't catch and Bill's wife then said, 'Come and sit by him, I'm sure it will help knowing you are there. I must telephone Mummy and speak to Michael, it's wonderful he's with her so I can be with darling Bill. Sister says he needs to feel we love him, however he is. Besides I must learn how I can best help him when he comes home.' That was it Mo, I remember every word. I couldn't go on sitting there. I told Tommy I'd made a mistake. He is so kind and let me be silent all the way back to London."

"Are you O.K.? Like another cuppa'?"

"Yes, I am all right, now." June smiled reassuringly. "It was awful being so near Bill, desperate to see him, and realising he did not need me. I knew I had no place there, seeing his wife and probably his parents made me realise I was the outsider. Before I ever got leave, Hemmy tried to point out the difference between friends and relatives when the chips are down. I must see Liz, and say how her mother was terrific. She knew exactly how I felt, but then she has lost a husband and is starting again." She put the empty mugs in the sink. "I'll have time to wash up in the morning. You must be dead-beat after that journey and me prattling on. I'll have to sort out the day's leave I haven't used, lucky really, as I need to go home and see what's up with Mum."

<u>Chapter Sixteen</u>

Catherine dreamed of Sam. She was building a sandcastle and the sea kept coming and washing it away. Sam would not help. He stood back, telling her it was useless. He walked away and she screamed, "Sam! Sam!" She woke, bedclothes on the floor, whispering his name.

Liz peered down. "What on earth? Was it a nightmare? I thought the bunk was going to take off."

"I was on the beach with Sam, he wouldn't help, he didn't want to know."

"Well I don't either. Go back to sleep. In case you've forgotten, it's our free morning, don't ruin our lie in." Liz burrowed under her bedclothes, seeking oblivion.

Catherine thought about the dream. Sam was on her mind, he was coming to the end of his project in London and she wished him to hurry back to the relative safety of Brighton, far away from the wretched doodlebugs. Sam's safety had taken precedence over worries for her Father fire watching in the City and Chris now back on the French coast.

Before going on watch at noon, she rang home. The telephone rang on and on. She pictured the empty hall and the jangling bell sounding from the shelf under the stairs.

"Sorry, I was in the garden." Alex sounded breathless. "Who's that? Oh Catherine. Why are you ringing? Anything wrong?"

"No, no, I'm O.K. here. I just wondered how everyone was, with the doodlebugs and everything." Her voice trailed off.

Alex, breath back, replied cheerfully. "Mum, Dad and me we're fine and Helen sounded jolly in her last letter, she's in Italy you know."

Catherine was maddened by his response. "What about Sam? Is he still in London?"

There was a pause and she heard Alex say, "It's Catherine."

"Darling, when are you coming home?" Her mother sounded enthusiastic. "We haven't heard from Sam lately. He should be home soon. Your father's very tired, there's been a lot of damage in London and travelling is a nightmare."

Catherine ended the conversation. She had no news of Sam and her mother had not listened to her.

"Stop worrying." Liz was firm as they pedalled down to the river. "Your mother would have known if there was anything really wrong."

They were kept busy all afternoon but by early evening the river had simmered down.

"Get some nosh while it's quiet," the Q.M. advised. "You'll need to standby later as a landing craft is due back. Don't know yet if the Yard wants them straight away or if they're to go on the buoys."

Petty Officer Pam greeted them at Pantiles. "Some man on a bike was asking for you." She looked curiously at Catherine. "He said Liz would do as well if you were busy some place."

Catherine could not think of any man cyclist who might be interested in her. "What does he look like?"

Pam was uncertain. "Not in uniform, not like anyone round here. Youngish and a bit rough, if you know what I mean."

"There you are." He pounced from behind. "I've been as far as the barrier enquiring for Tenant and Howard, the river heart breakers. A guard complete with rifle appeared out of a hut to get a good look at me. I suppose I could have been a Gestapo agent with designs on his smelly old sentry box, anyway he waved me away so here I am hot foot or rather pedal to the fountain head."

Sam, for the man was Sam, inclined his head to Pam in deference to her rank. "As I see, Ma'am, you have kindly collected the wanderers." Sam, astride his ancient bicycle, black hair on end, swung his rucksack from his shoulders and laughed at their amazement.

"He's my cousin." Catherine explained to Pam. "Don't tease Sam, what are you doing here?"

"Must say you look much more like a French collaborator than an enemy agent, you only need a string of onions and a black beret." Liz laughed out loud at the appearance of Catherine's eccentric cousin.

"Wipe off the surprise and joy, give us a welcome or better still, a cup of rosy lea. That saddle's a peculiar nasty torture, a few more miles and I'd have given away my grandma, if I had one."

Pam, unable to cope with such nonsense, excused herself.

Catherine and Liz smuggled Sam into the White House where he charmed the stewards for an extra supper.

"You still haven't told us why you are here." Catherine taxed him between mouthfuls of fish pie.

"London's full of bricks and mortar, up and down, and I just had a yen for the country before returning to Brighton for my final year at College. The lure of your river, not to mention your splendid company, was all the temptation I needed, and here I am."

"Yes, it's great, but what will you do while we're working?" Catherine looked at her watch, time to return to the river.

"He can come with us as a passenger." Liz suggested. "It'll give him a taste of the river."

"That might well be a fitting follow up to a fish pie." Sam had to add.

Stars were beginning to show in a darkened sky before the expected landing craft showed up. To Catherine's amazement it was Chris back again. She was conscious of Sam standing by the engine with Liz, deep in conversation, and wondered what he and Chris would make of each other.

Liz, when she recognised the numbers on the side of the craft, had similar thoughts. Chris, only in for a short time, would want all of Catherine, but Sam had come specially to see her. What did Catherine want? So much depended on what the cousins meant to each other.

Sam was keenly interested in the process of mooring up the landing craft. Catherine in command was a new experience for him. He was impressed by how well she and Liz worked together.

"What a carry on," he exclaimed, watching the sailors, on board the craft, take in the slack holding wire between the two giant buoys.

Catherine smiled, pleased with the completion of the exercise. "One ship's easy. It's when the whole flotilla wants attention, like yesterday, that the trouble starts." Her smile faded. "Sadly those days are over. Since D Day, the ships come in dribs and drabs and that can't change now."

The landing craft's side loomed above, casting a deep shadow into the cutter. Liz jabbed a stanchion and held on with her boathook. She called out to the fair-haired sub-lieutenant directing the crew.

"Hi Chris, great to see you back. Come and meet Catherine's cousin, he cycled by to see us."

Chris leaned over to grasp Sam's hand. His eyes were on Catherine and, even in the uncertain light, Sam saw the blush spread over her face. 'Wo, ho,' he thought: 'this young chap is special to Catherine.'

"Have you time between trips to come on board and welcome us home?" Jim, the skipper, appeared.

"Seen one of these tin cans before?" Jim took charge of Sam and led the way down to the wardroom. He removed the charts from the table and swept up the jumble of garments from the bunks. "Not much room and there's always a mess when we've been under passage." He yawned hugely, stretching his long arms up to the bulkhead. "Good to be back, the trip took forever with one dicey engine."

Catherine refused a second drink and reminded Liz they should be leaving for the next duty trip. Sam put down his empty glass, preparing to follow.

"No point in chugging up and down the river with the girls, why not hang on here until they've finished for the night." Jim enjoyed Sam's sharp humour. He reminded him of his own father, blinded in the First World War. It occurred to him that a nonsensical humour could cover a disability.

Waiting for the last passengers, Catherine considered where Sam could spend the rest of the night. "We can't smuggle him into Pantiles, no spare bunks and there'd be a colossal stink if he was caught."

Liz eyed the cutter. "Not very comfortable to sleep here."

Returning to pick up Sam, they found Jim had solved the problem. Chris waited for the cutter to come alongside. "Skip says he can stay and you are to pick him up sometime after eight. They are deep in argument over stresses and strains of the Forth Bridge, guess it'll go on to all hours." He leaned over and kissed Catherine's upturned face, cool in the night air. "We're not here for long but I should get ashore to morrow evening. Don't let's waste the time there is."

"Thank goodness Sam didn't seem to worry Chris. "Catherine announced as she and Liz waited on the moorings to be collected. "Mind you, it could be difficult if Sam stays on. I feel whacked, love is exhausting."

"Catherine, about Sam." The Pier head boat arrived and Liz lost the opportunity to ask Catherine exactly what she felt for Sam.

Sam was taken by the landing craft onto the slips in the Yard. He and Jim exchanged home addresses and Sam handed over the pencil sketch, he had drawn, of Jim in his wardroom, a goodwill gesture for bunk and breakfast. Jim's directions took him past the giant sheds and machine shops, across the Hard and onto the jetty. Catherine and Liz were busy cleaning the cutter for the next watch.

Liz gave the invitation casually. Catherine was enthusiastic. "Her grandparents live in a super old house. You would love it. Can't be far out of your way and nicer for Liz to have company since I can't go."

Liz said no more. She wanted him to agree but would not push.

Sam looked at Liz, trying to gauge if she had asked out of politeness and to suit Catherine. "Well thank you, if you are sure that's fine for you, Liz, and your folks won't mind?" He was relieved when she smiled her answer.

They took the route Liz knew so well, through winding lanes and small villages to her grandparents' home. It was her first visit since D Day, the country seemed strangely empty and she realised her grandparents would have lost their American guests.

Sam rode beside her, except when the way narrowed and then Liz led. He was a sympathetic listener, Liz told him a little of her childhood, her father and the sadness of his death. Sam responded by amusing her with a cameo of his own childhood. He delighted in her smile. He thought: 'She is beautiful. The whole combination makes a perfect girl. I want to paint her, capture her dark eyes, the lift of her chin and her flying curtain of hair.'

Colonel Howard was by the front door securing a branch of creeper and keeping a weather eye on the drive. The spaniels woke at the sound of wheels on gravel. The warning barks became an ecstatic welcome when Liz appeared. Sam caught her bicycle as she jumped down into her grandfather's arms and was startled to realise he was envious. The noise of the arrival brought Mrs Howard from the kitchen and Liz laughingly pulled Sam forward to be introduced.

"Liz, darling, you are so brown. I thought we'd have tea on the side lawn. Such a lovely day and the scones are ready." Mrs Howard looked at Sam, so thin with a pronounced limp. "You must be hungry." He needed looking after.

Tea over, Liz collected the chickens' eggs with her grandfather. Sam remained to string beans for supper with Liz's grandmother. He submitted to her grandmotherly interrogation with good grace. She found him easy company.

"Now the Americans have gone, we've shut off the top floor and my husband says I should ignore the rooms we don't use everyday in the rest of the house. I find that so difficult, it's been my only home all my married life. I like to keep it as well as I can but it is hard without servants." She stood up, easing her back. "That is lovely, thank you so much." She picked up the bowl of beans. "Of course this house is much too big for two old people on their own. It is good when Liz brings her friends. You must excuse me while I see to the evening meal."

Sam stood up. "Would you mind if I look round the outside of your beautiful home? It has such perfect Georgian proportions, lots of buildings of that period have been horribly messed with different owners popping on bits to suit themselves." He produced his sketch book from his pocket. "May I make a few drawings?"

Alice Howard loved her home to be appreciated and insisted on helping by bringing Sam a stool. Liz watched him, amazed by his speed and skill at representation. "I wish I could draw like that. I have tried the same view but can't get the lines right."

"Perspective is hard, but it can be learned." Sam noticed she had changed her uniform for a flowery cotton dress, accentuating her long legs. "What a fabulous house. You are so lucky to belong here." He left the stool, clumsily, and pulled her onto the grass. "Look, I'll give you a lesson on perspective."

Colonel Howard was in the study marking up his war map. It gave him great satisfaction to pierce Falaise with a red pin, signifying it was in Canadian hands following American and French troops landing in the South of France. He mused on the likelihood of his ex-lodgers involvement. The sound of voices and Liz's laugh floated through the window. He moved across the room to give the news of the fall of Falaise. Liz and Sam's dark heads were close together, bent over the sketch book. Sam held Liz's hand, guiding her pencil over the paper. It was plain that her eyes were on Sam not the paper.

"Hey, hey." Colonel Howard told himself: "It is not the moment for news of war."

Chapter Seventeen

Catherine chose a table at the end of the small garden behind the Duck and Feather. It was a warm evening and the smell of recently cut grass mingled with the heavy scent of tobacco plants and geraniums. She heard the distant chug of a duty boat returning down river mingling with the more immediate chatter of house martins as they swooped on insects for an evening meal. Monty, the pub cat, opened one eye when Catherine stroked him but was too lazy to move.

Chris threaded his way through the tables, careful not to spill the precious beer, and joined Catherine. He drank thirstily while she sucked in the froth to reach the bitter liquid. "Drink up or the wasps will get there first." He wiped his mouth with the back of his hand. "I'm going to get another, do you want the other half?"

Catherine shook her head, she had no capacity for beer, half a pint lasted her a whole evening. She watched Chris walk across the grass. Always thin, his uniform now hung loosely on his slight frame. She thought: 'Chris worries.' She knew he took his first lieutenant duties very seriously. Hating inefficiency, smooth running of the mess deck was everything to him. He had told her his aim was to be one of the best in the flotilla. Catherine had heard Jim advise: "Ease up on yourself, there's always tomorrow."

"Why does your cousin call you Cat?" Chris was back with a second pint.

"All my family call me Cat, can't remember anything different."

"Maybe that fits a little girl." He gave his lopsided grin. "I think Catherine suits you better, anyway Cat sounds spiteful." He took out his battered cigarette case. "Want a blue liner? It'll keep the midges away."

Catherine accepted a cigarette and they puffed companionably.

"Sam, your cousin, how does he know Liz?"

"We all met up in London, Sam was on his course and we were visiting Liz's mum." Catherine answered casually. "Sam's studying to be an architect." She wondered if Chris was jealous of Sam. "He's gone with Liz to meet her grandparents, they live in a super old house, not far."

A second atomic bomb was dropped on Nagasaki on the ninth of August, three days after the first. The destruction and loss of life was so great that the Japanese surrendered five days later. The World War was over. Clement Attlee announced September the second as V. J. Day, the official ending of hostilities.

"I shall be twenty in two months and I was thirteen when war was declared. All my growing up has been during a war," Catherine announced to Stephie as they prepared to go into Portsmouth and join in the celebrations.

"Leading Wren Tenant, there's a call for you," Quarters P.O. shouted up the stairs. "He says he'll hang on, but you'd better hurry. Take it in my office."

The office was empty. Catherine picked up the receiver, lying on the desk. "Hullo, this is Catherine, who am I speaking to?"

"Catherine, is it really you? I have been trying to track you down for ages, but you are always on the move." The voice was familiar but not enough to name. "Could we meet somewhere? I'm ringing from the Junior Officers' Club where I've a room for a couple of nights. I'm right at the end of my leave."

Catherine suddenly remembered; it was Jim Masters, Chris's ex C.O. "Jim?" she questioned, thinking: do I really want to meet him? I'm so much better about Chris. I might be disturbed all over again. But then, maybe he needs to see me. "Yes," she said uncertainly. "Yes, all right. I'll meet you in the bar at the J.O.C. in twenty minutes." She replaced the receiver without giving him a chance to reply.

Jim heard the line disconnect. The voice the other end sounded assured, not like the shy Catherine he remembered. He went to the bar, ordered a beer, chose a corner with a view of the door and began to think out what he should say.

"I don't want to keep him waiting; after all he is an old friend." Catherine looked at Stephie struggling into a cotton skirt and then critically at herself in the mirror. "This dress has turned out really well, you'd never guess it had been made out of old curtain material. But my mother is clever at this sort of thing." She picked up her uniform sling bag. "I'll try and meet up with you all before you leave the Queens' for the fair. If I don't make it, have a good time and don't do any thing I wouldn't."

"That gives me plenty of scope." Stephie was half serious. "Why don't you persuade Jim along too?"

The streets were crowded. The town was on holiday. Couples strolled through the gardens and dogs exercised their owners on the common where a gigantic bonfire had been prepared for the evening celebrations. Catherine could hear the noise of the fair in the distance. Slowing her pace, she approached the J.O.C. She stood at the swing door, hesitating, took a deep breath and pushed through. Jim was there, tall and thin with thick dark hair falling forward across his forehead. He stood, holding up his hand to catch her attention.

"Jim, have I kept you waiting?" Catherine smiled and dropped into the chair he had reserved. "Is that bitter you're drinking? A half would suit me."

Waiting to be served at the bar, he thought: 'She has the same cheeky grin, but so much more confidence'.

Catherine sipped the beer appreciatively and looked over the rim of her tankard. She thought: 'He is better looking than I remember, I'd forgotten his nose crinkled when he smiled.' She asked, "Where have you been and what have you been up to? It must be nearly a year since we've met".

"Is it as long as that?" he questioned, thinking: 'her eyes are the same, almost navy and she is attractive. I wish I was meeting her for the first time and she wasn't Chris's girl'. But he knew he could not shirk his task. He put down his beer. "I have been looking for you to say how terribly sorry I am about Chris." He paused; it was difficult to go on. "I can't help blaming myself for not knowing how ill he was. If only I had realised in time, I might have persuaded him to get to a medic earlier. Things could have been different; there would have been time to operate and he need not have died." He ran out of words, after all they weren't much use. He was prepared for her to slap his face, or walk out.

Catherine moved her chair closer and, to his astonishment, gave him a hug. "Jim, you are a darling. Thank you for coming and talking. It must have been awful, I mean the whole thing." She realised his hurt and feelings of guilt. "You know you shouldn't blame yourself, because Chris believed in being responsible for himself. He wouldn't have taken any notice of me or you or even his father if it hadn't been what he wanted."

"Well I do feel a louse, even so, but thank you for being so understanding." He took a gulp of beer and felt the prick of unshed tears and grasped her hand in the relief of telling. She let it stay warm and comforting within his.

They talked of the river and old times. Then they caught up on the last year. Catherine told Jim of Sam and Liz's engagement, of June going home to her family and the saga of Mo's father. Jim knew Dick was no longer involved with Mo and had guessed there was someone else, but not June's brother.

"What about you?" Jim could not help asking.

"Oh me, I just enjoy myself with anyone who turns up. I haven't wanted to get in deep." Catherine looked away sadly. "You know we are likely to be demobbed soon. There'll be no place for us when the men come back." Her eyes twinkled. "Our revered first officer told us boats crew wrens would not fit in with peacetime discipline."

"Have you any plans for when you're a civilian?" Jim wondered where he would find her. "I shall try to get into University. I was all set at the start of the war for an engineering degree but joined the R.N.V.R. instead."

"Well, I don't much care for the thought of returning home. My sister Helen is engaged to an Army chap she met in Italy; she won't be home for long and I'd rather not be there without her."

"Rumours are there'll be grants for ex service people. If so, I shall apply, my mother is a widow and couldn't possibly pay. You might get a grant yourself for a training."

They wandered out into the night and the lights of the big wheel at the fair beckoned. Catherine gasped at the view from the top. "Look," she directed Jim, "we can see all over Portsmouth and Southsea and those lights are at Ryde on the Isle of Wight". The wheel stopped and Jim slid his arm round her and it felt right. He tilted her face towards him and kissed her and that was right too.

The sky suddenly exploded into a myriad of breathtaking, coloured stars. "It sounds just like ack ack fire, but this is peace," Catherine murmured, inside Jim's arms. "So it's all over."

Jim looked down at her flushed face and saw the stars in her eyes. "It could be just beginning," he replied as the big wheel began to move, taking them slowly back to earth.